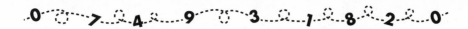

12 REAL-LIFE

MATH PROJECTS
KIDS WILL LOVE

by Todd Schroeder

SCHOLASTIC
PROFESSIONAL BOOKS

New York • Toronto • London • Auckland • Sydney
Mexico City • New Delhi • Hong Kong • Buenos Aires

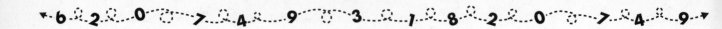

Acknowledgments

Thanks to my students, who have inspired me to develop these
materials by sharing their love of learning. Thanks to Jodi King, Jason Jansen,
and Mark Tank for guiding me with insights and suggestions to improve these
projects. Thanks to Janeal Lee for encouraging me to share this work with other
teachers. Thanks to Lisa Gies for allowing me to do great things for kids.
Thanks to the staff of J. R. Gerritts Middle School in Kimberly, Wisconsin,
for their commitment to kids and for making every day at work fun!
Finally, thanks to my wife Robyn and my sons, Cason and Andy,
who support me professionally and personally
every day of my life.

Cover design by Kelli Thompson

Cover art by Rich Harrington

Interior design by Sydney Wright

Interior illustration by Dave Clegg

ISBN: 0-439-36592-9

Copyright © 2003 by Todd Schroeder

Contents

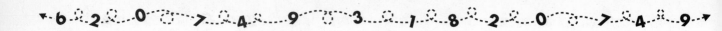
Introduction

Making Math Instruction "Real"

Can we ensure that each of our students becomes proficient in mathematics when we teach skills only in isolation? Of course not. Students need to learn—and are more interested in—skills that they will use in their daily lives. Too often we teach with explanation, practice, and memorization. When we teach math this way, we're asking students to learn unconnected bits of information. As a result, students have trouble internalizing skills and concepts, and learning becomes a struggle. Having students work on application-based activities like the ones in this book will help them not only practice math skills in context but also appreciate math as an important part of everyday real-life problem solving.

The Projects

The projects in this book can be used with fourth- through eighth-grade students, and tips for leveling the activities and for reaching multiple learning styles are provided throughout. Each project applies a wide variety of math concepts to problem-solving situations. In addition to applying key math skills, your students will learn to summarize, defend, evaluate, and communicate numerical information.

The activities in this book complement both traditional and non-traditional math programs.

Meeting the Standards

The activities are designed to meet the National Council of Teachers of Mathematics (NCTM) and National Economic standards; you will find a standards correlation grid on page 6. In addition to targeting the standards, these projects match the format and content of the applied problem-solving and free-answer response question sections on standardized tests. Using the reproducible pages may help familiarize your students with the types of short-answer and open-ended tasks they may encounter during the test.

Assessment

These activities can be assessed in a variety of ways, including traditional percentage, rubric evaluation, written feedback, and self-evaluation. A written assessment activity follows each project.

For the Teacher: A Walk-Through

Each project begins with a For the Teacher section. Following is an outline of some key elements you will find on these pages.

Required Skills

Students benefit most from these projects when they've already received instruction on the targeted math skills. For example, you would want to make sure that you had covered skill work on addition, subtraction, and multiplication of whole numbers and decimals before beginning The Checkbook Challenge (page 12), which strengthens and reinforces these basic math skills. Each project presents a variety of skills, providing reinforcement spiraling toward skill mastery.

Materials

These materials are required for or aid in the completion of the project.

Lesson Plan

This is a step-by-step time line that provides scope and sequence for the completion of the project. These four- to seven-day projects can be used with either block or traditional schedules, allowing for 45-minute class periods. However, you can easily adjust the time line to fit your curriculum and your students' needs. Review each project completely before you introduce it to your students, and be aware that you may need to spend one or two preparatory lessons introducing skills that are covered by the lesson, depending on your students' ability levels.

Teaching Tips

Because these projects come straight from my classroom, they have been teacher and student tested. From our work, I've developed tips that will help to ensure the successful completion of the projects. One management tip I recommend for all the projects is to have your students organize and label all scratch work in a math note-book. This makes finding computation mistakes much easier. Students who have no record of the equations they use to find answers become frustrated tracking down their mistakes.

Extend the Lesson

This section offers topics and ideas that are natural extensions of the project. It suggests ways to explore a skill in greater depth or introduce a new skill that is a spin-off of the activity.

Written Assessment

This concluding activity asks students to synthesize and apply the math skills and concepts they have learned outside the boundaries of the project to demonstrate how well they can communicate the meaning behind the numbers. Written assessment is also a required element on most standardized tests.

Correlation with the NCTM and National Economic Standards

Project and Page	Representation*	Connections*	Communication*	Reasoning and Proof*	Problem Solving*	Data Analysis and Probability	Measurement	Geometry	Algebra	Numbers and Operations	National Economic Standards
Fantasy Football Challenge ..7	•	•	•	•	•				•	•	Standard 7: Market forces; Standard 8: Law of supply and demand; Standard 13: Labor market; income
The Checkbook Challenge .12	•	•	•	•	•				•	•	Standard 2: Decision making; cost/benefit
An Investigation 19	•	•	•	•	•			•	•	•	Standard 7: Market forces; Standard 8: Law of supply and demand
The Stock Report 23	•	•	•	•	•			•	•	•	Standard 5: Exchange and trade
Number Theory Project ...31	•	•	•	•	•			•	•	•	
It's Payday! 39	•	•	•	•	•				•	•	Standard 13: Labor market; income
It's Tax Time 46	•	•	•	•	•			•	•	•	Standard 16: Income distribution; taxation
Take a Survey 54	•	•	•	•	•	•		•	•	•	Standard 14: Risk; profit; production
What's the Average? 62	•	•	•	•	•	•		•	•	•	
Take Your Best Guess 68	•	•	•	•	•	•		•	•	•	Standard 4: Responding to incentives
Games of Chance 73	•	•	•	•	•	•	•	•	•	•	
Home Design Project 81	•	•	•	•	•	•	•	•	•	•	Standard 2: Decision making; cost/benefit

* All the lessons in this book are grounded in these five standards. Each project requires students to encounter and find solutions to mathematical problems in terms of real-life situations (Connections and Problem Solving). The lesson extension activities and the written assessment activities provide opportunities for students to evaluate their learning and express their ideas with models and explanations that clearly communicate how they have solved a problem (Reasoning and Proof, Representation, Communication).

WEB LINKS
National Mathematics and Economic Standards

For a complete description of the National Council of Teachers of Mathematics Standards, go to **www.standards.nctm.org**. For a complete description of the National Council on Economic Education Standards, go to **www.economicsamerica.org/standards/contents.html**.

Fantasy Football Challenge

Students use computation, estimation, and planning skills to create their own fantasy football team by bidding on players and tracking their success.

About the Project

NCTM Standards

Numbers and Number Relationships, Number Systems and Number Theory, Computation and Estimation

National Economic Standards

Standards 7, 8, and 13

Required Skills

estimation
addition and subtraction of whole numbers
writing numbers in words

Materials

reproducibles (pages 9–11)
sports section of the Monday and Tuesday
   newspapers
football magazines or Internet

Before You Begin

▲ Students are excited about football at the beginning of the school year. Take advantage of their enthusiasm by doing this project to kick off the NFL season.

▲ Plan to start this project on the Thursday before any NFL regular season weekend and finish on the following Tuesday.

▲ Pick out up to 20 players' names for each position (QB = quarterback, RB = running back, WR = wide receiver/tight end,

K = kicker). You can determine the players who are up for auction using football magazines or the Web site **http://nfl.com**. NFL team rosters can be found in many football magazines and on the Internet. Students also have fun suggesting their own favorite players to include in the auction.

▲ On chart paper, post the names of players eligible for each position for students to review in advance of the auction.

▲ In the days before the auction, encourage your students to create a "dream team" of NFL players. This will get them thinking about what players they want to bid on.

Lesson Plan

Day 1 (Thursday)

Review the idea of a salary cap with your students and lay down the rules for the player auction. Using page 9 as a guide, conduct the auction. The bidding process will go faster if you allow multiple students to buy the same player. However, if students add to their rosters a player already chosen, they must pay an additional $250,000 above the winning bid. (For more tips on conducting the auction, see page 8.) Distribute copies of the Player Roster (page 9) and have students record the players they purchased. This will make tracking player statistics much easier.

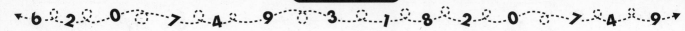

Day 2 (Friday)

Distribute copies of Players Under Contract on page 10. Have students complete this page in pen so they can't change players over the weekend.

Day 3 (Monday)

Some students will have players who are playing on Monday Night Football. As a result, their stat sheets can't be completed. Instead, have them complete the written assessment below or design a team helmet.

Day 4 (Tuesday)

Have students use the Monday and Tuesday sports page of the newspaper to tally how many points each of their players scored. Distribute copies of the Stat Sheet (page 11) and let students fill in this page, computing the fantasy points scored using the Point Values section. Rank the class teams in order of points scored.

TEACHING TIPS

- **Conducting the auction** is easy. Remind students that they must stay within their budgets (the combined salary of all the players on a team must be greater than $10,500,000 but no more than $18,000,000). Start by putting the name of an eligible quarterback up for bid. Begin the bidding at $100,000. Students can bid on players by raising their hands, increasing the money amount until only one student has his or her hand up. That student is the winning bidder and has the rights to that player. Allow other students to acquire the same player for an additional $250,000. This shortens the auction time. When every student has

picked a quarterback, start the bidding for the running back positions, beginning at $100,000 for each player making sure that students each acquire two running backs. Follow the same procedure for the three wide receiver/tight end positions and the kicker position to complete the roster.

- **Tell your students it's not necessary for them to watch the football games** in order to complete the project. They can find all the statistics they'll need using the Monday and Tuesday newspapers.

- **Reward the top teams!** Offer extra credit to the first-, second-, and third-place finishers.

Extend the Lesson

Some of your students may want to create a league and continue playing during the season. Help them set up a schedule so they can continue this activity on their own time.

Written Assessment

Ask students to respond to this prompt: Notice that the price of popular players went up as more people bid on them. Explain how supply and demand affects price.

 Fantasy Football Challenge

It's you against the other teams in the class! Can you pick the best team with a limited budget? Assemble a fantasy football team made up of seven players: one quarterback (QB), two running backs (RB), three wide receivers/tight ends (WR), and one kicker (K). Your entire team must fit within the salary cap rules.

How Your Players Score Points

Points are awarded according to the following rules: six points if your player scores a touchdown, three points if your player throws a touchdown pass, three points if your kicker gets a field goal, two points for a two-point conversion, and one point for an extra point (PAT). The team that scores the most points overall wins! If there's a tie, the team that has the lowest payroll is the winner.

Player Auction

Players for each position will be put up for auction. If you bid the highest for a player, add that player to your roster. If another student outbids you, don't worry! For an additional $250,000, you can add the same player to your roster. The bidding for each player starts at $100,000. The combined salary of all your players must be greater than $10,500,000 and no more than $18,000,000. Set a budget for how much you plan to spend on each player. This will help you stay within the salary cap rules. Good luck!

Player Roster

Estimated Spending for Players	**Actual Spending for Players**
QB $_____	QB $_____
RB $_____	RB $_____
RB $_____	RB $_____
WR $_____	WR $_____
WR $_____	WR $_____
WR $_____	WR $_____
K $_____	K $_____
Total $_____	Total $_____

Is the total team salary between $10,500,000 and $18,000,000?
YES or NO

Players Under Contract

List the players you have selected for your team. Give their salary both as a number and in words.

Example: QB *Michael Vick* _____ salary $ *5,260,500* _____

Five million two hundred sixty thousand five hundred dollars

QB _____ salary $ _____

_____ dollars

RB _____ salary $ _____

_____ dollars

RB _____ salary $ _____

_____ dollars

WR _____ salary $ _____

_____ dollars

WR _____ salary $ _____

_____ dollars

WR _____ salary $ _____

_____ dollars

K _____ salary $ _____

_____ dollars

Total Team Salary = $ _____ dollars

12 Real-Life Math Projects Kids Will Love   Scholastic Professional Books, 2003

Stat Sheet

Here's how to find the number of points your players scored. Check your players' performances in the sports section of Monday's or Tuesday's newspaper. (You may need both, depending on whether your players had games on Sunday or Monday.) In the box scores for NFL football games you'll find the number of touchdowns, touchdown passes, field goals, and extra points your players scored. Below, fill in the names of the players from your roster and calculate the points they scored. Then tally up your total score and compare with your classmates. The team that scores the most points overall wins! If there's a tie, the team that has the lowest payroll is the winner. Use the tiebreaker section to determine the winner.

Point Values:
Touchdown (running backs and wide receivers): 6 points
Touchdown pass (quarterback): 3 points
PAT—Point after attempt (kicker): 1 point
Two-point conversion (quarterback, running backs, wide receivers/tight ends): 2 points
Field goal (kicker): 3 points

The team that scores the most points overall wins! If there's a tie, the team that has the lowest payroll is the winner.

Player	**Points Scored**
QB _____	_____
RB _____	_____
RB _____	_____
WR _____	_____
WR _____	_____
WR _____	_____
K _____	_____

Tiebreaker

What is the difference between your team's salary and the salary cap amount ($18,000,000 dollars)? $ _____

Show your equation here:

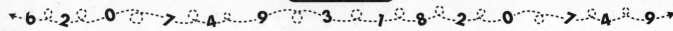

The Checkbook Challenge

Students complete a balance sheet and
write checks for financial transactions.

▲▲▲▲▲▲▲▲▲▲▲▲▲▲▲▲▲▲▲
About the Project
▼▼▼▼▼▼▼▼▼▼▼▼▼▼▼▼▼▼▼

NCTM Standards

Numbers and Number Concepts, Number
Systems and Number Theory, Computation
and Estimation, Patterns and Functions

National Economic Standards

Standard 2

Required Skills

estimation
addition, subtraction, and multiplication
   of whole numbers
addition, subtraction, and multiplication
   of decimals
writing numbers in words
calculating the percent of a number
rounding
determining least and greatest
place value

Materials

reproducibles (pages 15–18)
math notebook or scratch paper

▲▲▲▲▲▲▲▲▲▲▲▲▲▲▲▲▲▲▲
Lesson Plan
▼▼▼▼▼▼▼▼▼▼▼▼▼▼▼▼▼▼▼

Day 1

Generate a class discussion about how people
keep track of the money they earn and spend.
Using a transparency of the blank checks on
page 17, show the class how to write out a

check—this may be new for some students.
Introduce vocabulary that they'll encounter
during the lesson.

● transaction	Exchange; the act of spending or earning money
● debit	Money owed or spent
● credit	Money earned or gained
● balance	The total or difference after debit and credit transactions
● balance sheet	A sheet that helps you keep records of financial transactions
● sales tax	Tax added on to the purchase price of items you buy (you will use a 5% sales tax for this project)
● statement	A record the bank sends you that shows all your transitions for one month
● check	A written order instructing a bank to pay out money to a person or business

Day 2

Distribute copies of pages 16–18 to each
student, making sure to provide two copies of
page 17 (Checkbook) per student; they will
need to fill out six checks to complete the
project. Students complete transactions, the
balance sheet, and checks for days 1 to 14
(have students write the appropriate month in
the balance sheet).

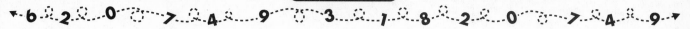
Day 3

Students complete transactions, the balance sheet, and checks for days 15 to 25.

Day 4

Students complete transactions, the balance sheet, and checks for days 27 to 29, calculate balance sheet totals, and complete the monthly statement.

Day 5

Students complete the optional written assessment activity below.

TEACHING TIPS

■ **Emphasize pencil-and-paper calculation.** Because this project is designed to reinforce the skills of addition, subtraction, and multiplication of whole numbers and decimals, students should make their calculations in a notebook or on scrap paper, rather than using calculators.

■ **Promote self-checking.** The correct balance answers are given for days 14 and 25. Students should check their subtotals against these answers, and locate their mistakes if the subtotals do not match. Allow students to find their own mistakes; this self-checking helps students as much as the actual calculations.

■ **Encourage a good habit.** Make sure students record all transactions on their balance sheets. Some students may point out that in a real checkbook cash transactions aren't recorded. You can assure them that this cash transaction record will help them figure out their true balance.

■ **Check for accuracy.** You can quickly evaluate students' understanding of place value and writing numbers in words by making sure the written and the numerical number match on the checks they've completed (page 17). This is a spiral review of a similar activity in the Fantasy Football project.

Extend the Lesson

Have your students use a balance sheet to record all the money they earn, spend, or are given for two weeks. Ask students to divide the items into two groups: things they want (candy, movies, games) and things they need (food, clothes). They can then determine what percent of their money went to unnecessary and to necessary items. Invite them to set a goal to spend less on luxury items over the next two weeks. Again, have them use a balance sheet to record all the money they earn, spend, or are given for the next two weeks and see if they can meet their budget goals.

Written Assessment

Effective decision-making requires comparing the additional costs with the additional benefits. Is there a point at which the cost of fixing a bike is not worth the value of the bike? What is that point—$1/4$ the value, $1/3$ the value, $1/2$ the value, or some other fraction? Defend and justify your answer, because your answer may differ from other students in class. Be sure to include the amount of money that would have been saved if you'd decided to buy a new bike sooner.

Answers

Page 16

Balance Sheet

Date	Transaction	Debit (-)	Credit (+)	Balance
____ 1	Beginning Balance		316.50	316.50
____ 2	Better Buys CDs	49.35		267.15
____ 2	Burger Chef lunch	5.65		261.50
____ 5	Smith baby-sit		29.05	290.55
____ 6	Candy Corner gumballs	3.15		287.40
____ 7	Clean room		10.00	297.40
____ 8	Kent's Bike Shop rim	36.72		260.68
____ 12	Sneakerlocker	68.09		192.59
____ 14	Mr. Ertl's leaves		28.75	221.34
____ 15	Kent's Bike Shop gears	57.35		163.99
____ 16	Crush cans		4.08	168.07
____ 17	Birthday gifts		97.00	265.07
____ 18	Jones baby-sit		25.80	290.87
____ 19	Kent's Bike Shop frame	37.42		253.45
____ 19	Tire World	11.33		242.12
____ 22	Dog-sit		15.75	257.87
____ 23	Kent's Bike Shop chain	10.35		247.52
____ 25	Sell bike		47.00	294.52
____ 27	Better Buys headphones	28.82		265.70
____ 29	Kent's Bike Shop bike	196.67		69.03
		Add all debits ⬇	Add all credits ⬇	Final balance from day 29
	Totals	504.90	573.93	69.03

Page 17

Check # 001
Better Buy: $49.35; Forty-nine ^{35}/100 Dollars

Check # 002
Kent's Bike shop: $36.72; Thirty-six ^{72}/100 Dollars

Check # 003
Sneakerlocker: $68.09; Sixty-eight ^{9}/100 Dollars

Check # 004
Kent's Bike Shop: $57.35; Fifty-seven ^{35}/100 Dollars

Check # 005
Kent's Bike Shop: $37.42; Thirty-seven ^{42}/100 Dollars

Check # 006
Kent's Bike Shop: $196.67; One hundred ninety-six ^{67}/100 Dollars

Page 18

1. 19	**7.** $141.84
2. Debit	**8.** $445.60
3. Day 29	**9.** $573.93
4. Day 1	**10.** $504.90
5. $54.85	**11.** $69.03
6. $600	**12.** $500.00

Balancing Your Checkbook

Are you ready to carry your own balance? Let's find out! You're going to balance a checkbook for one month's worth of transactions. You'll find a list of transactions to complete and checks to write below. You'll also receive a monthly statement to help you evaluate your income and expenses for the month.

Transactions

Using your checkbook and balance sheet, make and record the following transactions. Round all tax answers to the nearest hundredth. Enter all transactions on the balance sheet, including both *(check)* and *(cash)*.

> Tip: To figure out the tax, multiply the price by the percentage of tax in decimal form: Price x 5% Tax (5.00 x 0.05)= $0.25. Total cost = $5.25

Day 1   The beginning balance in your checkbook is $316.50

Day 2   You buy four CDs at a cost of $11.75 each at Better Buys. Add 5% tax. *(check)*

Day 2   You buy lunch at Burger Chef for $5.65 *(cash)*

Day 5   You baby-sit the Smith kids for seven hours. The Smiths pay you $4.15 per hour.

Day 6   You buy nine gumballs at the Candy Corner at $0.35 each. *(cash)*

Day 7   Your parents pay you $10.00 for keeping your room clean this month.

Day 8   You run your bike into a curb and wreck the front wheel and rim. Repairs at Kent's Bike Shop cost you $13.25 for labor and $22.35 for parts. Add 5% tax only on the parts. *(check)*

Day 12 You buy a new pair of basketball shoes at the Sneakerlocker that cost $64.85. Add 5% tax. *(check)*

Day 14 You rake leaves for Mr. Ertl for five hours. He pays you $5.75 per hour.

Day 15 The gears on your bike are rusted and need to be replaced. You have work done at Kent's Bike Shop, costing $36.40 for labor and $19.95 for parts. Add 5% tax on parts only. *(check)*

Day 16 You cash in 136 aluminum cans and earn $0.03 for each can.

Day 17 It's your birthday! You receive gift money from these members of your family: $35.00 from your older brother, who just got a job; $30.00 from your grandma; $12.00 from your aunt Martha, who collects beads; and $20.00 from your crazy uncle from upstate.

Day 18 You are paid $4.30 per hour for six hours of baby-sitting for the Jones family.

Day 19 Dad runs over your bike in the driveway. Repairs to straighten your bike frame at Kent's Bike Shop cost $37.42. *(check)*

- 6 2 0 7 4 9 3 1 8 2 0 7 4 9 →

Day 19 You pay to have your dad's flat tire patched at Tire World. The repairs cost $9.70 for labor and $1.55 for the patch. Add 5% tax on the patch. *(cash)*

Day 22 You are paid $3.15 per hour for taking care of the neighbor's dog for five hours.

Day 23 The chain breaks on your bike. You buy a new chain at Kent's Bike Shop that costs $9.86. Add 5% tax. *(cash)*

Day 25 You sell your bike to a friend for $47.00.

Day 27 You buy a set of headphones at Better Buys for $27.45. Add 5% tax. *(cash)*

Day 29 You buy a new mountain bike at Kent's Bike Shop that cost $187.30. Add 5% tax. *(check)*

Balance Sheet

Date	Transaction	Debit (-)	Credit (+)	Balance
____ 1	Beginning Balance		316.50	316.50
____ 2				
____ 2				
____ 5				
____ 6				
____ 7				
____ 8				
____ 12				
____ 14				221.34
____ 15				
____ 16				
____ 17				
____ 18				
____ 19				
____ 19				
____ 22				
____ 23				
____ 25				294.52
____ 27				
____ 29				
		Add all debits ⬇	Add all credits ⬇	Final balance from day 29
	Totals			

12 Real-Life Math Projects Kids Will Love Scholastic Professional Books, 2003

6 2 0 7 4 9 3 1 8 2 0 7 4 9

Checkbook

Use these checks to pay for the transactions requiring a check.

You will need two pages of checks to complete this project!

Bank of the Fox River   Check # _____
123 Any Street   Date _____ 20 ___
Mytown, USA 90210

Pay _____ $ _____

_____ Dollars

Memo _____   _____ (Signature)

Bank of the Fox River   Check # _____
123 Any Street   Date _____ 20 ___
Mytown, USA 90210

Pay _____ $ _____

_____ Dollars

Memo _____   _____ (Signature)

Bank of the Fox River   Check # _____
123 Any Street   Date _____ 20 ___
Mytown, USA 90210

Pay _____ $ _____

_____ Dollars

Memo _____   _____ (Signature)

Monthly Statement

Answer these questions using information from the balance sheet. Complete this page after you have finished balancing your checkbook (page 16).

1. How many total transactions did you make? _____

2. Did you make more credit or debit transactions? _____

3. On what day was your balance the lowest? _____

4. On what day was your balance the highest? _____

5. How much money did you make baby-sitting this month? _____

6. Using your answer from question 5, round to the nearest ten dollars. How much money would you make baby-sitting during an entire year? _____

7. Including tax, how much money did you spend on bike parts and labor for the repairs? _____

8. What was the total amount of money paid out by check? _____

9. What is the total of your Credit column? _____

10. What is the total of your Debit column? _____

11. What was the difference between the total of all the credit and debit transactions? _____

12. Estimate by rounding to the nearest hundred dollars the total amount you spent this month. _____

12 Real-Life Math Projects Kids Will Love   Scholastic Professional Books, 2003

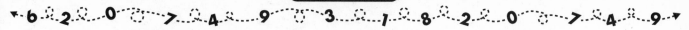

An Invest-igation

Students purchase stocks and calculate
their growth and decline over time.

About the Project

NCTM Standards

Number and Number Concepts, Number
Systems and Number Theory, Computation
and Estimation, Patterns and Functions

National Economic Standards

Standards 7 and 8

Required Skills

estimation
rounding
addition, subtraction, and multiplication of
    mixed decimals
division of whole numbers
decimal/percent conversions
integers

Materials

reproducibles (pages 21–22)
business section of the newspaper or
    business Web sites

Note: Yahoo.com has an outstanding stock
market Web site, **http://finance.yahoo.com**.
Students can use this site to find letter prefixes
for companies, research their performance, and
track stock prices in real time. Line graphs for
all stocks are also provided, which can add
visual support to discussions about range, patterns, and trends in stock prices.

Before You Begin

▲ Set aside one or two lessons for selecting
stocks, determining purchase shares, and
introducing vocabulary. Plan one lesson to
teach how to fill out the Invest-igating the
Stock Market report, which can then be
repeated regularly throughout the year.

Lesson Plan

Days 1 and 2

Use the business section of a newspaper or a
stock market Web site (see Materials) to open a
discussion about selecting and buying stocks.
Students are usually excited to see stock prices
in real time on the Internet.

As a class, decide on ten stocks that students
are interested in. Narrow this down to three
companies the class wants to invest in with
$9,000. Have students find the current stock
prices of these companies and work backward
to determine how many shares they can
purchase of each one. Note that they must
invest less than 50 percent of the money in
any given stock—a parameter that offers you
the opportunity to talk with students about
wise investing practices.

Encourage students to spend as much of the
$9,000 as they can. They should record the
unspent money as an initial loss. If there
is an overall loss in the stocks, they will need
to add this initial loss figure to the total loss
figure in question 2 before they calculate the
percent loss in question 3.

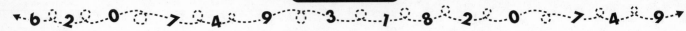
Day 3

Distribute copies of Invest-igating the Stock Market (page 22). Make sure students have Invest-igation Vocab on hand for reference.

Have students fill in the information from the stock selections they've made. They should include the names and stock symbols of each company, the number of shares they have "purchased," and the purchase price for each stock. Finally, they will calculate the percentage of gain or loss per share (total gain or loss divided by 9,000 = percent gain or loss) and answer the questions about gains and losses below the chart. You can complete this as a group activity, using the newspaper or a Web site to provide students with the current value of each stock.

Day 4 and beyond

You can make this a real-life, ongoing activity by assigning students to keep track of stock prices over time. Create a master copy of the Stock Holdings chart (page 22), which records the initial number of shares purchased and their purchase prices for each stock the class selected. Copy and distribute the page when you assign the activity. Students will use the initial data for all other Stock Reports they complete during the year.

This ongoing report makes a terrific activity anytime during the school year, and using it at natural breaks in my curriculum has worked well. You might consider handing it out before vacations, and it's a good project to leave for a substitute.

■ **Mimic the market.** While this activity can be completed using either fractions or decimals, point out to students that the stock market currently uses decimals.

■ **Teach integers.** Stocks that lose value give you an outstanding opportunity to discuss integers. Show how you can get a negative answer to a subtraction problem.

Extend the Lesson

▲ Have students create a line graph to record the growth and decline of their stocks over time. This makes a striking class bulletin-board display.

▲ Start an investment competition for students or classes. Who can earn the greatest percent increase in the price of his or her stock? Who can gain the most money?

▲ Have students discuss the purpose of adding positive and negative numbers together in a stock situation (e.g., the total value of stock holdings per share for these three stocks: +.80, +2.57, and –5.35 would be –1.98). This is a required skill in algebra with real-world applications in the stock market.

Assessment

There are ten total answers for the students to find. This includes the current stock values, gains or losses per share, and the three questions below the chart. Assign a point total for each answer.

Written Assessment

Give students the following assignment: Write a letter to a company requesting a stock report, brochure, or year-end report. Analyze the report with an adult and write about what you learned about the company's performance and stock value.

6 2 0 7 4 9 3 1 8 2 0 7 4 9

Invest-igation Vocab

Here are some helpful terms and equations to help you track your stock performance in the market!

stock   Ownership of a corporation that is represented by shares

share   Certificate representing ownership in a corporation

transaction   The act of buying or selling shares of stock

investing   Buying shares of stock in order to make a profit

price   The amount of money each share of stock is worth

purchase price   The amount of money each share of stock is worth at the time of purchase

current price   The amount of money each share of stock is worth now

current value   The amount of money all the shares of a stock are worth now

     Number of shares owned x Current price of the stock = Current value

loss   A decrease in the value of a stock, lower than the purchase price; the loss is not realized until the stock is sold

     Purchase price – Current price = Loss
(if the stock value has decreased)

gain   An increase in the value of a stock, higher than the purchase price; the gain is not realized until the stock is sold

     Current price – Purchase price = Gain
(if the stock value has increased)

percent gain/ loss   How much the value of the stock has increased or decreased as a percentage of the amount invested

     Total gain or loss ÷ the amount invested ($9,000) = Percent gain or loss

⇅ Invest-igating the Stock Market ⇅

What does it mean to have a gain or loss in your stock shares? Try investing $9,000 in three companies you believe are performing well. Then track their performance to see if the shares you purchased gained in value or decreased in value. Did you make a choice that earned or lost money?

Guidelines

▲ Start out with $9,000 dollars to invest.

▲ Choose stocks from three different companies to invest in.

▲ Find the price used for each stock on the Internet or in the business section of the newspaper and record that in the Purchase Price column below.

▲ Figure out how many shares of each company's stock you can purchase for $9,000. Divide the shares in the best way you can to invest all your money at the start. Any money you do not invest will be considered an initial loss. (Note: the maximum amount for an individual stock investment is 50% of $9,000.)

Stock Holdings

Name and Symbol of Company	Number of Shares	Purchase Price	Current Price	Current Value	Gain or Loss Per Share
Current Value of all stocks (add all three current values)	⟶				⟵

1. What is the current value of all stocks rounded off to the nearest whole number?   _____

2. Using your answer from question 1, what is the total gain or loss from $9,000 for all your stocks?   _____

3. What is the percent gain or loss for all your stocks, rounded to the nearest tenth of a percent?   _____ %

12 Real-Life Math Projects Kids Will Love   Scholastic Professional Books, 2003

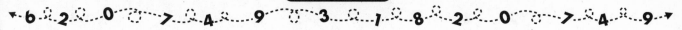

 # The Stock Report

(challenging)

Students calculate the value of stocks for a small stock portfolio
and display the growth and decline of stock values on a line graph.
They find number patterns and make informed predictions based on these patterns.

About the Project

NCTM Standards

Numbers and Number Concepts, Number Systems and Number Theory, Computation and Estimation, Patterns and Functions

National Economic Standards

Standard 5

Required Skills

add, subtract, multiply fractions and
 mixed numbers
integers
display data on a line graph
determine the pattern in numbers
make predictions given number patterns
inequalities
determine the range of a graph

Materials

reproducibles (pages 27–30)
business section of the newspaper or
 business Web sites
colored pencils

Before You Begin

▲ In the weeks before you begin this project, have your students bring in articles or news clippings about stocks or the stock market. Discuss the workings and vocabulary of the stock market (for a kid-friendly overview of the history and function of the stock market,

see **www.themint.org**). Building prior knowledge helps correct students' misconceptions and helps them develop a basic knowledge of finance.

▲ Use the Invest-igation Vocab sheet (page 21) to help students review the following vocabulary: stock, share, gain, loss. New terms to introduce include:

• dividend	A cash payment using company profits that is distributed to the stockholders. Dividends may be in the form of cash, stock or property.
• range	The difference between a stock's low price and high price during a trading period
• trend	The general direction of a stock's price

Lesson Plan

Day 1

Tell students that they are going to build a stock portfolio based on their knowledge of the stock market and watch their investments grow! Using examples of companies students are interested in from the business section of the newspaper, or business Web sites such as **http://finance.yahoo.com**, guide your students through sample problems to help them understand when and how to use the

equations introduced in this project and listed below. (Note: the nine-year investment example reflects the scenario students will encounter on the reproducible pages of this activity.)

- Year 1 value = Year 1 stock price x Number of shares owned

- Year 9 value = Year 9 stock price x Number of shares owned

- Total dividend = Stock dividend x Number of shares owned

- Total current value = Year 9 value + Total dividend value

- Gain or loss = Year 9 stock value − Year 1 stock value

Day 2

Distribute copies of the reproducibles and review the project with students: They will evaluate the growth patterns of four different stocks in their imaginary portfolio. Show them how to use the Your Portfolio section (page 27) and Tracking Stock Prices chart (page 28) to calculate the total dividends for each stock, and fill out the Profit and Loss Statement (page 30) for Reiss Steamship and Interlake.

As students examine the Tracking Stock Prices chart, point out that today, the stock market uses decimals for stock prices. In the past, however, values were listed as mixed numbers and fractions. Explain that because these stocks were purchased nine years ago, mixed numbers and fractions are used.

Day 3

Have students calculate the dividends and complete the Profit and Loss Statement for Huron Cement and Seaprint.

Day 4

Read the information about price patterns on page 28 with students and show them how to evaluate the Tracking Stock Prices chart. They should use the information from the chart to predict the price direction for each stock in years 10, 11, and 12 and complete the questions at the bottom of the page. Then they can plot price patterns for all four companies' stocks on the graphs on page 29. (Note: Students who are stronger visual learners may benefit from completing the graphs first so they can see the patterns before answering the questions.)

Day 5

Have students use their completed charts and graphs to answer the questions on the Profit and Loss Statement. Pose the question from the top of page 27: Should you hold, sell, or buy more of these stocks? Students should be able to give the following responses: Sell Reiss Steamship; its price trend is down. Hold or buy more Interlake; its price trend is up. The price pattern for Huron shows hold for one year, then sell. Hold Seaprint; its price is flat, but yields high dividends.

TEACHING TIPS

- **Emphasize pencil-and-paper calculation.** Because this project is designed to reinforce the skills of addition, subtraction, and multiplication of mixed numbers and fractions, students should make their calculations in a notebook or on scrap paper, rather than using calculators.

■ **Create easy-to-read color line graphs.**
It's easier for you to evaluate the line graphs
if your students use colored pencils to
complete them. Encourage them to use a
different color to represent each stock.

■ **Justify predictions.** The class may have a
variety of correct answers for their price
predictions. Explain that their predictions
need to be within an acceptable range of
values (see Answer Key, page 26). Some
students will argue that because these are
predictions, they can't be wrong. Emphasize
that because there is a pattern to the values,
answers that do not follow the pattern are
considered incorrect.

■ **Post the equations.** Write the equations
on page 24 on chart paper. Students will
be more successful when you post the
equations used for the project in your
classroom. Guide your students through
sample problems to help them understand
when and how to use these equations.

Extend the Lesson

You can introduce algebra and using variables
in equations by having students calculate the
current price of a stock given the total value
and the number of shares owned.

Example: $166 \frac{1}{2} = C \times 37$

C is the current price, $166 \frac{1}{2}$ is the total
value, and 37 is the number of shares of stock
owned. The current price for this problem is
$4\frac{1}{2}$ or $4.50.

Written Assessment

Explore with your class the differences among
terminating, non-terminating, and repeating
decimals in their calculations for this project.
What are the implications of rounding money
amounts to the nearest hundredth? Have
students respond to the following problem:
The stock market now uses decimals to
represent stock values in fractions. For
example, .50 has replaced $\frac{1}{2}$ to represent
a half dollar. This change causes a problem
with fractions like $\frac{1}{3}$ because non-terminating
repeating fractions have no exact decimal
equivalent. Explain the problem that results in
converting these fractions to decimals and
discuss possible solutions. Give examples of
other fractions that create this problem.

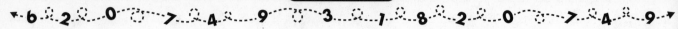
Answer Key

Page 28

(Determine the Price Patterns)

Reiss Steamship: Fall; $0–3

Interlake: Rise; $20–24

Huron Cement: Fall; $4–8

Seaprint: Stay about the same; $7–10

Page 29

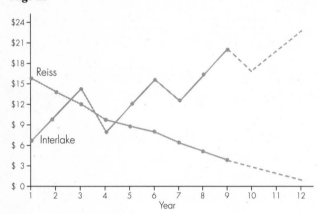

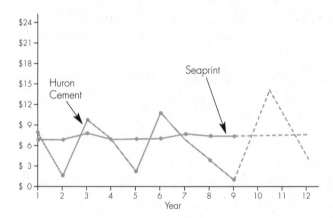

Page 30

Stock Name	Total Value Year One	Total Value Year Nine (Current Value)	Total Amount of Dividends	Total Value With Dividends	Total Amount of Gain or Loss
Reiss Steamship (14 shares)	231	$50\frac{3}{4}$	0	$50\frac{3}{4}$	$-180\frac{1}{4}$
Interlake (18½ shares)	$124\frac{7}{8}$	$349\frac{23}{24}$	$41\frac{5}{8}$	$391\frac{7}{12}$	$+266\frac{17}{24}$
Huron Cement (10¾ shares)	86	$14\frac{1}{3}$	$59\frac{1}{8}$	$73\frac{11}{24}$	$-12\frac{13}{24}$
Seaprint (8⅓ shares)	$61\frac{11}{24}$	$68\frac{1}{3}$	125	$193\frac{1}{3}$	$+131\frac{7}{8}$
Totals	$503\frac{1}{3}$	$483\frac{3}{8}$	$225\frac{3}{4}$	$709\frac{1}{8}$	$+205\frac{19}{24}$

1. Interlake $+226\frac{17}{24}$
2. Seaprint $+131\frac{7}{8}$
3. Reiss Steamship $-180\frac{1}{4}$
4. Huron Cement $-12\frac{13}{24}$
5. Reiss Steamship: range of $12\frac{7}{8}$
6. Seaprint: range of $1\frac{3}{20}$
7. Interlake
8. Reiss Steamship, Huron Cement
9. Seaprint

The Stock Report

You just might be RICH! Nine years ago, you were given shares of four different stocks. Should you hold, sell, or buy more of these stocks? It is your decision to make. Use your research skills to find current and past values, predict future prices, and make your decision.

You share ownership of these stocks with other people. For example, you may own seven and one half shares of a particular stock. This means you own seven full shares, but the eighth share is divided between you and another person.

Your Portfolio

14   shares of Reiss Steamship
18 ½   shares of Interlake
10 ¾   shares of Huron Cement
 8 ⅓   shares of Seaprint

> *Hint: When calculating the total value of the stock, multiply the number of shares owned by the price of the stock.*
> - *Year 1 value = Year 1 stock price x Number of shares owned*
> - *Year 9 value = Year 9 stock price x Number of shares owned*

Some companies give dividends to stock owners. Dividends are much like interest on a savings account—the company gives you money in return for your investment. Below are the dividends earned per share of stock during the entire nine-year period.

Stock Dividend

Reiss Steamship	$ 0 per share	(14 shares owned)
Interlake	$ 2 ¼ per share	(18 ½ shares owned)
Huron Cement	$ 5 ½ per share	(10 ¾ shares owned)
Seaprint	$ 15 per share	(8 ⅓ shares owned)

> *Hint: To find the amount of dividend for each stock, multiply the dividend by the number of shares owned.*
> - *Total dividend = Stock dividend x Number of shares owned*

6 2 0 7 4 9 3 1 8 2 0 7 4 9

Tracking Stock Prices

Year one is the year the stocks were bought. The chart below shows the purchase price for each stock. Year nine represents the current price for each stock.

Name of Stock (Number of shares)	Purchase Prices								
	Year One	Year Two	Year Three	Year Four	Year Five	Year Six	Year Seven	Year Eight	Year Nine
Reiss Steamship (14 shares)	$16\frac{1}{2}$	$14\frac{1}{4}$	12	$10\frac{3}{8}$	$9\frac{1}{8}$	$7\frac{3}{4}$	$6\frac{7}{8}$	5	$3\frac{5}{8}$
Interlake (18 $\frac{1}{2}$ shares)	$6\frac{3}{4}$	$10\frac{5}{12}$	$14\frac{1}{2}$	$8\frac{1}{2}$	$12\frac{2}{3}$	16	$12\frac{4}{9}$	$16\frac{1}{4}$	$18\frac{11}{12}$
Huron Cement (10 $\frac{3}{4}$ shares)	8	$2\frac{1}{3}$	$9\frac{3}{10}$	$6\frac{2}{5}$	$2\frac{1}{2}$	$11\frac{5}{6}$	$6\frac{1}{3}$	$4\frac{1}{2}$	$1\frac{1}{3}$
Seaprint (8 $\frac{1}{3}$ shares)	$7\frac{3}{8}$	8	$8\frac{2}{5}$	$8\frac{1}{4}$	$7\frac{3}{10}$	$7\frac{1}{4}$	$7\frac{3}{5}$	$7\frac{1}{4}$	$8\frac{1}{5}$

Determine the Price Patterns

Some stock prices show a pattern over time. For example, a stock's price may rise for two years, fall for one year, rise for two years, and so forth. From this pattern you can make a prediction whether a stock's value will rise or fall during a given year. Using the chart above, identify the pattern for each stock during this nine year period. Assume the patterns you discover continue without change when you make your predictions.

1. Predict the price direction for each stock from year nine to year twelve. Will it rise, fall or stay about the same between those years? Circle your answer in the chart below.

2. What price do you predict each stock will be at for year twelve? Fill in the chart with your prediction.

Stock	Predicted Growth (circle one)	Year Twelve Prediction
Reiss Steamship	Rise Fall Stay about the same	Predicted price = _____
Interlake	Rise Fall Stay about the same	Predicted price = _____
Huron Cement	Rise Fall Stay about the same	Predicted price = _____
Seaprint	Rise Fall Stay about the same	Predicted price = _____

12 Real-Life Math Projects Kids Will Love Scholastic Professional Books, 2003

6 2 0 7 4 9 3 1 8 2 0 7 4 9

Graphing Stock Prices Over Time

Make a line graph for each stock that shows its growth and decline in price over time. Make price predictions by extending the graph to years 10, 11, and 12. When making these predictions, you should assume that past price patterns continue without change. You can label and display two stocks on each graph by using different colored pencils for each stock.

> HINT: Use the data from the Tracking Stock Prices chart to complete these graphs.

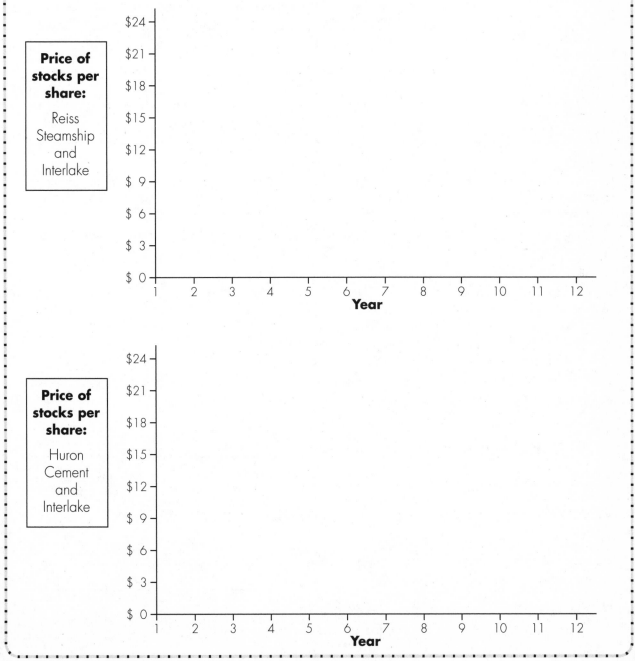

Price of stocks per share:

Reiss Steamship and Interlake

Price of stocks per share:

Huron Cement and Interlake

6 2 0 7 4 9 3 1 8 2 0 7 4 9

Profit and Loss Statement

Use these equations to complete the Profit and Loss Statement below.

- Year 1 value = Year 1 stock price x Number of shares owned
- Year 9 value = Year 9 stock price x Number of shares owned
- Total dividend = Stock dividend x Number of shares owned
- Total current value = Year 9 value + Total dividend value
- Gain or loss = Year 9 stock value − Year 1 stock value

Stock Name	Total Value Year One	Total Value Year Nine (Current Value)	Total Amount of Dividends	Total Value With Dividends	Total Amount of Gain or Loss
Reiss Steamship (14 shares)					
Interlake (18½ shares)					
Huron Cement (10¾ shares)					
Seaprint (8⅓ shares)					
Totals					

Use the profit and loss statement above and line graphs on page 29 to answer these questions.

1. Which stock has the greatest gain from year 1 to year 9 with the dividends included? _____ How much?_____

2. Which stock has the smallest gain from year 1 to year 9 with the dividends included? _____ How much?_____

3. Which stock has the greatest loss from year 1 to year 9 with the dividends included? _____ How much?_____

4. Which stock has the smallest loss from year 1 to year 9 with the dividends included? _____ How much?_____

5. Which stock has the largest range in price? _____ How much?_____

6. Which stock has the smallest range in price? _____ How much?_____

7. Which stocks do you predict will rise in value by year 12 compared to year one? _____

8. Which stocks do you predict will fall in value by year 12 compared to year one? _____

9. Which stocks do you predict will have little or no change in value by year 12 compared to year one? _____

12 Real-Life Math Projects Kids Will Love   Scholastic Professional Books, 2003

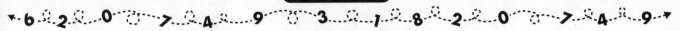

Number Theory Project

Students display knowledge of
number theory concepts by finding and
explaining their answers to non-traditional problems.

About the Project

NCTM Standards

Numbers and Number Concepts, Number
Systems and Number Theory, Computation
and Estimation, Patterns and Functions,
Algebra

Required Skills

factors
multiples
prime numbers
composite numbers
prime factorization
exponents
expanded notation
square roots
cubed roots
order of operation for equations
fractions

Materials

reproducibles (pages 34–38)

Before You Begin

▲ Check the types of problems presented on
the reproducible pages of this project to
make sure that students are familiar with
number theory skills that are presented.

Lesson Plan

Day 1

Introduce the project to your students as a
series of mini-challenges to review and
reinforce their grasp of number theory
concepts. Distribute copies of By the Numbers
(page 34) and have students complete this
warm-up. As you review the answers, be sure
to discuss the meanings of terms such as
common factor, *multiples*, *prime numbers*,
composite numbers, *factorization*, *exponents*,
expanded notation, and *square root*.

Day 2

Distribute copies of page 35 and guide students
through the Sieve of Eratosthenes. This activity
demonstrates the use of multiples and square
roots to find prime numbers.

Share this information with the class: In about
200 B.C. the Greek mathematician Eratosthenes
devised an algorithm for calculating prime
numbers. Eratosthenes discovered that
because 2 is prime, then all multiples of 2 are
composite (an integer exactly divisible by at
least one other number than itself and 1).
The same is true for 3, 5, 7, and so on. He
then discovered that square roots can be used
to determine a stopping point for finding prime
numbers. For example, in order to find the
prime numbers under 100 quickly, you can
cross out all the multiples (composites) of the
numbers less than or equal to 10 and greater
than 1 (2, 3, 4, 5, 6, 7, 8, 9, and 10). All

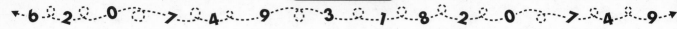

numbers remaining on the chart that are not crossed out are prime. Why? The greatest number being tested as prime is 100 and the square root of 100 is 10. You can stop at the greatest square root. Have students complete the Sieve of Eratosthenes up to 100.

You can use a transparency of page 35 or a laminated hundreds chart to review the answers. (For a step-by-step demonstration of the Sieve of Eratosthenes, see **http://ccins.cam osun.bc.ca/~jbritton/jberatosthenes.htm**, and for an interactive version of the Sieve of Eratosthenes, visit **http://www.faust.fr.bw. schule.de/mhb/eratosiv.htm.**)

Day 3

Distribute copies of page 36. Have students identify from the set of given numbers a number that doesn't belong in the group and explain their reasoning. Answers may vary for each question. For example, in the number set (5, 15, 20, 35, 45, 58) 5 is the only prime number. However, 58 is the only number that isn't a multiple of 5, and 20 is the only number that doesn't have a face value of 5. Encourage students to find more than one solution to each set of numbers. If students work in groups, let them earn 10 points for each initial answer (total score: 70) and 2 or 3 points for each additional solution, based on the sophistication of the class.

Day 4

Distribute copies of page 37 and have students identify a pattern in each set of numbers. They should give the next number in the pattern and write a defense of their answer on the lines below. (Be aware that there is only one correct answer to these questions.) You may want to point out that example 6 (0, 1, 1, 2, 3, 5) represents the Fibonacci numbers. You can help students apply this pattern to examples

in nature (rabbits, cows, and seashells!) by visiting **http://www.mcs.surrey.ac.uk/ Personal/R.Knott/Fibonacci/fibnat.html**.

Day 5

Distribute copies of page 38 and ask students to apply the rules for the order of operations to create an equation that makes each statement true. For example:
54 12 3 = 6 is 54 ÷ (12 − 3) = 6

■ **Scaffold problem solving with hints.**
When students experience trouble finding solutions to the number patterns, support them with hints such as, "Think about exponents in this problem," or "This problem uses multiples." This provides them with alternative paths without giving away the answer.

Extend the Lesson

Use the Web site **http://www-groups.dcs. st-and.ac.uk/~history/BiogIndex.html** to research historical mathematicians. You may want to direct students first to biographies of Eratosthenes and Fibonacci, whose discoveries are highlighted in this project.

Written Assessment

Have students research a mathematician from the above Web site. Assign this activity: Write a short report to share with the class about the contribution your mathematician made to math. What important math concept did he or she discover?

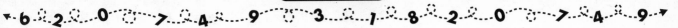
Answer Key

Page 34

1. 1, 2, 3, 4, 6, 8, 12, 16, 24, 48
2. 1, 2, 3, 4, 6, 12
3. 4
4. 2
5. 6, 12, 18, 24, 30, 36, 42, 48
6. 60, 120, 180
7. 24
8. 48
9. 2, 3, 5, 7, 11, 13, 17, 19
10. 3 or more
11. 2
12. $2^2 \times 3^2$
13. $2^2 \times 17$
14. $2^2 \times 3 \times 5$
15. $3^2 \times 5^4 \times 7$
16. 2^9
17. $3 \times 3 \times 3 \times 3 = 81$
18. $2 \times 2 \times 2 \times 3 \times 3 \times 7 \times 7 = 3{,}528$
19. 12
20. 10

Page 35

1	2	3	4	5	6	7	8	9	10
11	12	13	14	15	16	17	18	19	20
21	22	23	24	25	26	27	28	29	30
31	32	33	34	35	36	37	38	39	40
41	42	43	44	45	46	47	48	49	50
51	52	53	54	55	56	57	58	59	60
61	62	63	64	65	66	67	68	69	70
71	72	73	74	75	76	77	78	79	80
81	82	83	84	85	86	87	88	89	90
91	92	93	94	95	96	97	98	99	100

(Circled numbers: 2, 3, 5, 7, 11, 13, 17, 19, 23, 29, 31, 37, 41, 43, 47, 53, 59, 61, 67, 71, 73, 79, 83, 89, 97)

1. When finding the prime numbers under 100, you cross out all the multiples of the numbers less than or equal to 10 because they are all composite. The numbers 2, 3, 5, and 7 are the prime numbers less than 10. Because 10 is the square root of 100, it is the stopping point when finding prime numbers less than 100. All numbers remaining that are not crossed out are prime.
2. 10
3. 2

Page 36

Answers may vary. Responses should include a logical reason for excluding the circled number.

Page 37

1. 14; This is the next even number.
2. 49; This is the next multiple of 7.
3. 17; This is the next prime number.
4. 128; The next number is the last number times 2.
5. 43; This is the next twin prime.
6. 13; The next number is the sum of the last two numbers. (Fibonacci numbers)
7. 15; This is the next composite number.
8. 65,536; The next number is the square of the last number.
9. 1,944; The next number is the product of the last two numbers.
10. 49; This is the next perfect square.

Page 38

1. $(17 - 3) \div 7 = 2$
2. $5 \times (3 + 2) = 25$
3. $10 - (40 \div 8) = 5$
4. $42 \div 6 + 3 \times 1 = 10$
5. $(12 - 4) \div (2 \times 2) = 2$
6. $20 + 8 \div 4 - 4 = 18$
7. $17 + 4 \times 2 + 2 = 27$
8. $2 \times (8 - 1) \times 2 = 28$
9. $(5 + 8 \times 2) \div 7 = 3$
10. $(6 + 3) \times (4 + 2) = 54$

By the Numbers

See how many of the following challenges you can answer!

1. List all the factors of 48. _____

2. List the common factors of 24 and 36. _____

3. List the greatest common factor (GCF) of 32 and 60. _____

4. List the greatest common factor (GCF) of 20 and 42. _____

5. List the first 8 multiples of 6. _____

6. List the first 3 common multiples of 15 and 20. _____

7. List the least common multiple (LCM) of 8 and 12. _____

8. List the least common multiple (LCM) of 16 and 24. _____

9. List all the prime numbers less than 20. _____

10. How many factors do composite numbers have? _____

11. How many factors do prime numbers have? _____

12. Give the prime factorization with exponents of 36. _____

13. Give the prime factorization with exponents of 68. _____

14. Give the prime factorization with exponents of 60. _____

15. Simplify this equation using exponents: _____
$3 \cdot 3 \cdot 5 \cdot 5 \cdot 5 \cdot 5 \cdot 7$

16. Simplify this equation using exponents: _____
$2 \cdot 2 \cdot 2 \cdot 2 \cdot 2 \cdot 2 \cdot 2 \cdot 2 \cdot 2$

17. Give the expanded equation and answer for 3^4. _____

18. Give the expanded equation and answer for: _____
$2^3 \cdot 3^2 \cdot 7^2 =$

19. What number is the square root of 144? _____

20. What number is the square root of 100? _____

12 Real-Life Math Projects Kids Will Love   Scholastic Professional Books, 2003

Name _____ Date _____

Sieve of Eratosthenes (1 to 100)

Cross out all composite numbers and circle all the prime numbers up to 100 on the chart below.

Composite number: a number with three or more factors. For example, 25 is a composite number with the factors 1, 25, and 5.

Prime number: a number with only two factors: 1 and itself. For example, 3 is a prime number with the factors 1 and 3.

1	2	3	4	5	6	7	8	9	10
11	12	13	14	15	16	17	18	19	20
21	22	23	24	25	26	27	28	29	30
31	32	33	34	35	36	37	38	39	40
41	42	43	44	45	46	47	48	49	50
51	52	53	54	55	56	57	58	59	60
61	62	63	64	65	66	67	68	69	70
71	72	73	74	75	76	77	78	79	80
81	82	83	84	85	86	87	88	89	90
91	92	93	94	95	96	97	98	99	100

1. How is the square root of a number the key to the Sieve of Eratosthenes and finding prime numbers? _____

_____

_____

2. At what number can you stop testing numbers when finding the primes to 10? _____

3. At what number can you stop testing numbers when finding the primes to 400? _____

Which Number Doesn't Belong?

Circle the number that doesn't belong in each set. Defend your choice with a short written response. Your answer should include a mathematical reason for excluding the number you choose.

1. 6   12   22   29   38   50

_____

_____

2. 15   33   55   87   93   99

_____

_____

3. 3   7   11   15   31

_____

_____

4. 5   15   20   35   45   58

_____

_____

5. $1/4$ $3/5$ $2/6$ $7/9$ $2/9$ $1/5$

_____

_____

6. 4.5   2.53   19.5   5.9   .517

_____

_____

7. .15 $3/2$ 150% $1\frac{1}{2}$

_____

_____

Challenge:

6^2 $4 + 5 \times 4$ $144/4$ 36 $2^2 \times 3^3$

_____

_____

12 Real-Life Math Projects Kids Will Love   Scholastic Professional Books, 2003

Which Number Comes Next?

Determine the next number in the sequence or pattern. Defend your choice with a short written response. Explain the sequence or pattern in each number set.

1. 2   4   6   8   10   12   ____

_____

2. 7   14   21   28   35   42   ____

_____

3. 2   3   5   7   11   13   ____

_____

4. 2   4   8   16   32   64   ____

_____

5. 11   13   17   19   29   31   41   ____

_____

6. 0   1   1   2   3   5   8   ____

_____

7. 4   6   8   9   10   12   14   ____

_____

8. 2   4   16   256   ____

_____

9. 2   3   6   18   108   ____

_____

10. 1   4   9   16   25   ____

_____

Complete the Equations

Use any of the mathematics operation symbols [+ − x ÷ ( )] to make all of the equations true statements. Always apply the order of operation rules for equations.

For example: 54   12   3 = 6   is   54 ÷ (12 − 3) = 6

1.   17   3   7 = 2

2.   5   3   2 = 25

3.   10   40   8 = 5

4.   42   6   3   1 = 10

5.   12   4   2   2 = 2

6.   20   8   4   4 = 18

7.   17   4   2   2 = 27

8.   2   8   1   2 = 28

9.   5   8   2   7 = 3

10.   6   3   4   2 = 54

12 Real-life Math Projects Kids Will Love Scholastic Professional Books, 2003

It's Payday!

Students determine work time
on the job and complete paychecks with
withholdings for four employees.

About the Project

NCTM Standards

Numbers and Number Concepts, Number
Systems and Number Theory, Computation
and Estimation, Patterns and Functions,
Measurement

National Economic Standards

Standard 13

Required Skills

calculate elapsed time to the nearest minute
make percent/decimal conversions
find the percent of a number
add and subtract decimals
round decimals to the nearest hundredth
write numbers as words

Materials

reproducibles (pages 42–45)

Before You Begin

▲ Help familiarize students with paychecks
and withholdings by letting them visit the
IRS Web site TAXinteractive at
**www.irs.gov/individuals/page/0,,id=1554
8,00.html**. This site provides student-
friendly definitions and examples of jobs
teens might have. It also includes cool
cartoon graphics.

Lesson Plan

Day 1

Tell students they will get to play the part of a
business manager over the next few days.
During this time they will be responsible for
using different pay rates and time cards to
determine exactly how much each of their four
employees receives in his or her paycheck.

Distribute copies of pages 42–44 and review
the business terms (*withholdings*, *gross pay*, *net
pay*, *overtime*, *pay period*) and related equations
and business math vocabulary outlined on
page 42. You may also need to review the
terms listed under "Withholdings For All
Employees" and explain why employers are
required to take money out of their employees'
paychecks for federal taxes, state taxes, and
social security, and where those withholdings go.

Discuss the different time intervals that
businesses use when paying their employees.
Explain that some businesses pay weekly, some
pay biweekly, and others pay monthly. Show
your students how to calculate elapsed time
on a time card. (The tips on adding time and
working with units of time in decimals on
page 42 provide students with some helpful
explanations and examples.)

Day 2

Have students complete time cards for Ed Gott
and George Slone (page 43). Make sure they
understand how to figure out overtime hours

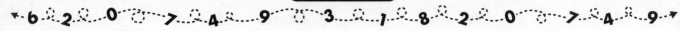

(hours worked beyond the 40 regular hours). Remind them to use decimals to record their answers.

Day 3

Have students complete time cards for Kaye Barker and Jane Cowling (page 44). Review time card answers for all four employees before moving on to the next step.

Day 4

Distribute two copies of pages 45 to each student. Have students complete the payroll checks for Ed Gott and George Slone. Make sure they have copies of the completed time cards on hand for reference. You may want to model how to fill out the first check using an overhead transparency of page 45. Students will need to calculate the gross pay (Gross pay = Hours worked x Pay per hour) and then the amount of each withholding category (Amount withheld = Tax percent x Gross pay). Finally, they should find the total amount of money withheld and determine the net pay (Net pay = Gross pay – Total withholding).

Day 5

Have students complete checks and pay stubs for Kaye Barker and Jane Cowling.

Day 6

Assign the optional written assessment at the end of this lesson.

TEACHING TIPS

■ **Check for accuracy.** Correct your students' time cards for all four employees before they calculate gross pay for the payroll checks (Day 3) to ensure they are working with accurate data. Also, be sure to correct your students' gross pay amounts before they complete the pay stubs. Accurate totals are needed in order to calculate the proper withholding amounts.

Extend the Lesson

Our counting system is base 10, but the counting system for time is base 60. This is an opportunity for you to discuss counting in different bases with your students.

Written Assessment

Have students respond to this payroll scenario: The business manager is considering options for an increase in work hours. Five additional hours will be added to the work schedule. She is going to give the five hours to Ed Gott as overtime hours instead of hiring a new employee who would earn $10.65 per hour. She has chosen this option because she thinks it is cheaper. The business manager has made a mistake in her thinking. Explain what her mistake is. Defend your opinions with mathematical evidence.

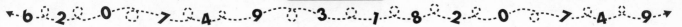

Answer Key

Pages 43–44

Ed Gott
Week one: Mon: *8hr 45min* Tues: *6hr* Wed: *7hr 45min*
Thu: *8hr 30min* Fri: *9hr 15min*; Total: *43hr 15min*
Week two: Mon: *8hr 15min* Tues: *9hr 30min* Wed: *9hr 15min*
Thu: *10hr 45min* Fri: *7hr 30min*; Total: *45hr 15min*
Week one regular work hours: *40*
Week one overtime work hours: *3hr 15min*
Week two regular work hours: *40 hr*
Week two overtime work hours: *5hr 15min*

George Slone
Week one: Mon: *9hr 15min* Tues: *8hr 15min* Wed: *7hr*
Thu: *8hr 30min* Fri: *7hr 45min*; Total: *40hr 45min*
Week two: Mon: *8hr 30min* Tues: *6hr 30min* Wed: *6hr 45min*
Thu: *9hr 30min* Fri: *8hr*; Total: *39hr 15min*
Week one regular work hours: *40 hr*
Week one overtime work hours: *45min*
Week two regular work hours: *39hr 15min*
Week two overtime work hours: *None*

Kaye Barker
Week one: Mon: *8hr 45min* Tues: *8hr* Wed: *6hr* Thu: *8hr 30min*
Fri: *8hr 15min*; Total: *39hr 30min*
Week two: Mon: *7hr 30min* Tues: *9hr 30min* Wed: *8hr 45min*
Thu: *5hr 30min* Fri: *6hr 30min*; Total: *37hr 45min*
Week one regular work hours: *39hr 30min*
Week one overtime work hours: *None*
Week two regular work hours: *37hr 45min*
Week two overtime work hours: *None*

Jane Cowling
Week one: Mon: *6hr 45min* Tues: *7hr 15min* Wed: *6hr*
Thu: *7hr 30min* Fri: *8hr 30min* Total: *36h*
Week two: Mon: *7hr 15min* Tues: *7hr 30min* Wed: *6hr* Thu: *8hr 30min* Fri: *6hr 30min*; Total: *35hr 45min*
Week one regular work hours: *36hr*
Week one overtime work hours: *None*
Week two regular work hours: *35hr 45min*
Week two overtime work hours: *None*

Bank of Fox River
123 Any Street
Mytown, USA 90210

Date _____ 20 __

Pay *Ed Gott* _____ (Employee name)

four hundred ninety-three 90/100 _____ Dollars

Check #001

_____
(Your signature)

Withholding Amounts

Federal income tax (8.6%) = *$56.63*   State income tax (5.05%) = *$33.26*

Social Security (6.75%) = *$44.45*   Retirement contribution (2%) = *$13.17*

Health insurance (2.2%) = *$14.49*   Holiday Club (.4%) = *$2.63*

Gross pay = *$658.53*   Total withholding = *$164.63*   Net pay = *$493.90*

Bank of Fox River
123 Any Street
Mytown, USA 90210

Date _____ 20 __

Pay *George Slone* _____ (Employee name)

seven hundred fifty-three 52/100 _____ Dollars

Check #001

_____
(Your signature)

Withholding Amounts

Federal income tax (8.6%) = *$86.40*   State income tax (5.05%) = *$50.74*

Social Security (6.75%) = *$67.82*   Retirement contribution (2%) = *$20.09*

Health insurance (2.2%) = *$22.10*   Holiday Club (.4%) = *$4.02*

Gross pay = *$1,004.69*   Total withholding = *$251.17*   Net pay = *$753.52*

Bank of Fox River
123 Any Street
Mytown, USA 90210

Date _____ 20 __

Pay *Kaye Barker* _____ (Employee name)

five hundred eighty-four 2/100 _____ Dollars

Check #001

_____
(Your signature)

Withholding Amounts

Federal income tax (8.6%) = *$66.97*   State income tax (5.05%) = *$39.32*

Social Security (6.75%) = *$52.56*   Retirement contribution (2%) = *$15.57*

Health insurance (2.2%) = *$17.13*   Holiday Club (.4%) = *$3.11*

Gross pay = *$778.68*   Total withholding = *$194.66*   Net pay = *$584.02*

Bank of Fox River
123 Any Street
Mytown, USA 90210

Date _____ 20 __

Pay *Jane Cowling* _____ (Employee name)

three hundred forty-one 17/100 _____ Dollars

Check #001

_____
(Your signature)

Withholding Amounts

Federal income tax (8.6%) = *$39.12*   State income tax (5.05%) = *$22.97*

Social Security (6.75%) = *$30.71*   Retirement contribution (2%) = *$9.10*

Health insurance (2.2%) = *$10.01*   Holiday Club (.4%) = *$1.82*

Gross pay = *$454.90*   Total withholding = *$113.73*   Net pay = *$341.17*

💲 It's Payday! 💲

It's payday, and your job as business manager is to calculate employees' pay! Some businesses use time cards to keep track of how much their employees earn. You will be working with business terms and equations to calculate the correct amount for each check.

Business Terms and Equations

withholdings (includes taxes, insurance, social security, and retirement)
Money taken out and subtracted from a person's paycheck. This includes taxes, insurance, social security, and retirement.

gross pay The amount of pay before any withholdings are subtracted.
Gross pay is calculated by this equation: Gross pay = Hours worked x Pay per hour.

net pay The amount of money an employee receives. Net pay is calculated by this equation: Net pay = Gross pay − Total of all withholdings.

overtime Time worked over the regular 40-hour work week. The overtime pay rate is called "time and a half" which means an employee making $5.00 per hour is paid $7.50 for each hour worked over the regular 40.

pay period Some pay periods cover two weeks, or 80 hours. There are two time cards for each employee, one for each week. Both cards are used to calculate an employee's pay for one pay period.

Business Math Employers Need to Know

Rounding decimals Since our money system doesn't go beyond the hundredth place value, you'll need to round all decimals to the nearest hundredth.

Adding time in our base 10 counting system Time is a base 60 counting system. Adding time is different than adding numbers.
For example, 30 + 35 = 65 but 30 minutes + 35 minutes = 1 hour and 5 minutes.

Working with units of time in decimals Find the decimals for time by dividing the number of minutes by sixty. For example: 15 min = 15 ÷ 60 = .25 of an hour. Fifteen minutes is equal to one fourth (a quarter) of an hour.

Withholdings for All Employees
Federal Income Tax = 8.6%
State Income Tax = 5.05%
Social Security = 6.75%
Retirement Contribution = 2%
Health Insurance = 2.2%
Holiday Club = Different for each person

Hourly Pay Rates
George Slone = $12.50 per hour
Kaye Barker = $10.08 per hour
Ed Gott = $7.10 per hour
Jane Cowling = $6.34 per hour

12 Real-Life Math Projects Kids Will Love   Scholastic Professional Books, 2003

- 6 - 2 - 0 - 7 - 4 - 9 - 3 - 1 - 8 - 2 - 0 - 7 - 4 - 9 -

Time Cards

Fill out these time cards to determine how many regular and overtime hours employees Ed Gott and George Slone worked over a two-week period. Make sure to use decimals to record your answers.

Ed Gott $7.10 per hour

Week One

Day	Start	Finish	Hours Worked
MON	7:45 A.M.	4:30 P.M.	_____
TUES	8:00 A.M.	5:00 P.M.	_____
WED	7:45 A.M.	3:30 P.M.	_____
THU	8:10 A.M.	4:40 P.M.	_____
FRI	7:30 A.M.	4:45 P.M.	_____
Total work hours: Week one =			_____

Week Two

Day	Start	Finish	Hours Worked
MON	7:45 A.M.	4:00 P.M.	_____
TUES	7:30 A.M.	5:00 P.M.	_____
WED	7:15 A.M.	4:30 P.M.	_____
THU	8:00 A.M.	6:45 P.M.	_____
FRI	7:15 A.M.	2:45 P.M.	_____
Total work hours: Week two =			_____

George Slone $12.50 per hour

Week One

Day	Start	Finish	Hours Worked
MON	6:45 A.M.	4:00 P.M.	_____
TUES	9:00 A.M.	5:15 P.M.	_____
WED	7:45 A.M.	2:45 P.M.	_____
THU	7:40 A.M.	4:10 P.M.	_____
FRI	8:30 A.M.	4:15 P.M.	_____
Total work hours: Week one =			_____

Week Two

Day	Start	Finish	Hours Worked
MON	9:45 A.M.	6:15 P.M.	_____
TUES	7:30 A.M.	2:00 P.M.	_____
WED	6:45 A.M.	1:30 P.M.	_____
THU	7:15 A.M.	4:45 P.M.	_____
FRI	7:45 A.M.	3:45 P.M.	_____
Total work hours: Week two =			_____

	Week One	Week Two
Regular work hours =	_____	_____
Overtime work hours =	_____	_____

	Week One	Week Two
Regular work hours =	_____	_____
Overtime work hours =	_____	_____

6 2 0 7 4 9 3 1 8 2 0 7 4 9

$ Time Cards $

Fill out these time cards to determine how many regular and overtime hours employees Kaye Barker and Jane Cowling worked over a two-week period. Make sure to use decimals to record your answers.

Kaye Barker $10.08 per hour

Week One

Day	Start	Finish	Hours Worked
MON	12:45 P.M.	9:30 P.M.	_____
TUES	1:00 P.M.	9:00 P.M.	_____
WED	1:45 P.M.	7:45 P.M.	_____
THU	2:10 P.M.	10:40 P.M.	_____
FRI	7:30 A.M.	3:45 P.M.	_____

Total work hours: Week one = _____

Week Two

Day	Start	Finish	Hours Worked
MON	12:45 P.M.	8:15 P.M.	_____
TUES	12:00 P.M.	9:30 P.M.	_____
WED	1:45 P.M.	10:30 P.M.	_____
THU	1:55 P.M.	7:25 P.M.	_____
FRI	7:40 A.M.	2:10 P.M.	_____

Total work hours: Week two = _____

Jane Cowling $6.34 per hour

Week One

Day	Start	Finish	Hours Worked
MON	1:45 P.M.	8:30 P.M.	_____
TUES	2:00 P.M.	9:15 P.M.	_____
WED	1:45 P.M.	7:45 P.M.	_____
THU	12:15 P.M.	7:45 P.M.	_____
FRI	7:20 A.M.	3:50 P.M.	_____

Total work hours: Week one = _____

Week Two

Day	Start	Finish	Hours Worked
MON	2:15 P.M.	9:30 P.M.	_____
TUES	12:30 P.M.	8:00 P.M.	_____
WED	1:30 P.M.	7:30 P.M.	_____
THU	12:10 P.M.	8:40 P.M.	_____
FRI	7:30 A.M.	2:00 P.M.	_____

Total work hours: Week two = _____

	Week One	Week Two
Regular work hours =	_____	_____
Overtime work hours =	_____	_____

	Week One	Week Two
Regular work hours =	_____	_____
Overtime work hours =	_____	_____

12 Real-Life Math Projects Kids Will Love Scholastic Professional Books, 2003

6 2 0 7 4 9 3 1 8 2 0 9

$ **Payroll Checks** $

You will need two pages of checks to complete this project!

It's time to pay your employees for their two weeks of work. Use their regular and overtime hours and pay rates to determine their gross pay. Use the withholding percentages below to find out how much to deduct (total withholding) from their gross pay. Once you've subtracted the total withholding from their gross pay, you have net pay, the actual amount you will pay them.

Bank of Fox River
123 Any Street
Mytown, USA 90210

Date _____ 20 ___

Pay _____ (Employee name)

_____ Dollars

Check #001

_____
(Your signature)

Withholding Amounts

Federal income tax (8.6%) = _____   State income tax (5.05%) = _____

Social Security (6.75%) = _____   Retirement contribution (2%) = _____

Health insurance (2.2%) = _____   Holiday Club (.4%) = _____

Gross pay = _____   Total withholding = _____   Net pay = _____

Bank of Fox River
123 Any Street
Mytown, USA 90210

Date _____ 20 ___

Pay _____ (Employee name)

_____ Dollars

Check #001

_____
(Your signature)

Withholding Amounts

Federal income tax (8.6%) = _____   State income tax (5.05%) = _____

Social Security (6.75%) = _____   Retirement contribution (2%) = _____

Health insurance (2.2%) = _____   Holiday Club (.4%) = _____

Gross pay = _____   Total withholding = _____   Net pay = _____

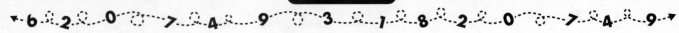

It's Tax Time

Students complete a state and federal
tax return for a family of five.

About the Project

NCTM Standards

Numbers and Number Concepts, Number
Systems and Number Theory, Computation
and Estimation, Patterns and Functions

National Economic Standards

Standard 16

Required Skills

addition, subtraction, and multiplication of
    whole numbers and decimals
calculating the percent of a number
percent/decimal conversions
rounding
determining inequalities

Materials

reproducibles (pages 49–53)
calculator

Before You Begin

▲ Make sure students are familiar with the way
    withholdings are placed on most paychecks
    to cover federal and state taxes. (You may
    want to preface this in-depth tax project
    with the It's Payday! project, page 39.)

Lesson Plan

Day 1

Lead your students in a discussion about taxes
and tax forms. Explore reasons taxes are
needed by the government and how they're
collected. Spark students' interest by handing
out real forms that are available at any U.S.
post office. Introduce the following vocabulary:

• withholding	An amount of money kept by the government used to pay for personal taxes
• tax credit	An amount of money that is subtracted from a person's taxable income
• itemized deduction	An amount of money subtracted from a person's taxable income for donations of money or property given to a charity

Distribute copies of page 49 and review
with students the activity scenario: They are
accountants who must prepare a tax return for
a family of five. Discuss any unfamiliar vocabulary and point out how page 49 provides the
data they will need to complete the rest of the
activity. Ask students whether they think the
family will owe taxes or have overpaid and
accrued enough expenses that they will receive
a refund.

Day 2

Distribute copies of pages 50–53 and have students compare the state and U.S. tax forms. They should look at the lengths of the forms and details of the entries.

Guide students through the first few questions of the State Tax Form OK-EZ to help them get started. Make sure to correct students' answers as they finish because they will need to use information from the state return on Schedule A: Itemized Deductions and on Form 1040 U.S. Income Tax Return. Checking for accuracy at this step prevents mistakes from being compounded later.

Note: For students who are just beginning to learn about taxes, you may want to stop the project here and have them try filling out the State Tax Form OK-EZ again with a new family tax scenario and income data. The next four days of work with itemized deductions and the federal income tax form are challenging.

Day 3

Have students complete page 53 (Schedule A: Itemized Deductions.) Correct their answers as they finish because they will need accurate information from the Itemized Deduction return to complete Form 1040 U.S. Income Tax Return.

Days 4 and 5

Have students complete pages 51–52, Form 1040 U.S. Income Tax Return. Check answers and review students' findings. Did the family owe taxes or did they overpay?

Day 6

Have students complete the written assessment activity at the end of this lesson.

TEACHING TIPS

■ **Calculators minimize difficult work with percentages.** Because this project emphasizes percent and decimal conversions and calculating percentages, you may want to allow students to use a calculator. However, you should emphasize pencil and paper work if students need extra work on computation skills.

■ **Deadline: April 15.** Doing this project in late March or early April will increase student interest and motivation. The topic of taxes and tax returns will be in the news and is reinforced at home by those parents who prepare their own taxes.

Extend the Lesson

Taxes are used to pay for government services. The value of these services to the public should outweigh the cost. In a class discussion, have your students list services that the government provides and pays for. Examples include police and fire protection, schools, parks, libraries, and roads. Have your students classify these services as either *essential* or *quality of life* items. Lead a discussion about which category public libraries fall under. Some may argue that because taxpayers can buy books at a store, libraries aren't worth the cost. This type of civics debate gives you an opportunity to teach math across the curriculum, and could be an additional written activity.

Written Assessment

Have students respond to the following scenario: A businessperson wants a special deal on property taxes from the local government. Instead of paying $100,000, he wants to pay only $25,000. If this happens,

he promises that his company will add twenty employees at an average income of $40,000 each. He points out that the local government collects 15 percent of employee income as taxes. Will the local government collect more money than it loses on this deal? Show proof that the man's reasoning is or is not correct.

Answer Key

Page 50

1. $ 56,425
2. $ 27
3. $ 67
4. $ 295
5. $ 56,814
6. $ 150
7. $ 2,633
8. $ 1,136
9. $ 3,919
10. $ 52,895
11. $ 6,876
12. $ 4,232
13. $ 316
14. $ 4,548
15. $ 2,328
16. $ 2,257
17. None
18. $ 71

Pages 51–52

1. $ 56,425
2. $ 27
3. $ 67
4. $ 295
5. $ 56,814
6. $ 600
7. $ 4,500
8. $ 4,961
9. $ 12,439
10. $ 22,500
11. $ 34,314
12. $ 8,235
13. $ 1,500
14. None
15. $ 2,257
16. $ 521
17. $ 4,278
18. $ 3,957
19. $ 3,668
20. None
21. $ 289

Pages 53

1. $ 3,825
2. $ 2,938
3. (Students will use the minimum deduction since line 2 is less than 12% of $30,000 or $3,600)
4. $ 600
5. $ 1,650
6. $ 2,850
7. $ 4,500
8. (Students will use the line 7 total since it is greater than 6% of $30,000 or $1,800)
9. $ 4,500
10. $ 2,328
11. $ 2,633
12. $ 4,961
13. $ 4,020
14. $ 707
15. $ 5,712
16. $ 2,000
17. $ 12,439
18. $ 22,500

It's Tax Time

It's tax time, and you're the accountant! Your task is to prepare a tax return for a family of five. The parents, Bob and Judy Woodward, have three children: Lori (3), Sara (7), and Todd (14). All the financial information that you need is provided below. As you organize the materials, you may find that some data will not be used.

Income For the Year

Wages
Bob $21,645
Judy $34,780

Investment income
Savings interest..............$27
CD interest $67
Stock dividend $295

Expense Receipts This Year

Donations
Church.................$1,200
  (Gift of money)
Cancer Fund $200
  (Gift of money)
Firefighter's Fund $250
  (Gift of money)
Donated car..........$2,850
  (Gift of property)

Child Care
Kinder Care $4,020

Retirement Investment
IRA Fund...............$2,000

Medical & Dental Expenses
Children's
Hospital $3,635
Dental Plaza............$190

Local Property Tax Paid
Tax bill $1,470
School assessment...$1,163

Home Mortgage Interest Paid
First NA Bank........$5,712

Job Expenses
Mileage $47
Clothing $185
Union Dues..............$475

W4 Withholding Statement
(Current percentages being withheld)

State withholding
4% of income...........$2,257

Federal withholding
6.5% of income   . . .$3,668

Other Directions

Round off all money totals to the nearest dollar (whole number) when necessary.

6 2 0 7 4 9 3 1 8 2 0 7 4 9

State Tax Form OK-EZ

1. Wages . . . .$ _____

2. Interest on savings . . . .$ _____

3. Interest on CD's . . . .$ _____

4. Dividends from stock . . . .$ _____

5. Add lines 1 through 4 (This is the amount of your taxable income) . . . .$ _____

6. Dependent deduction. Number of children (under 18) = ___ x $50 =. . .$ _____

7. Property tax deduction (property tax paid this year) = ...$ _____

8. Married couple deduction 2% of line 5 (Round to the nearest dollar) . . . . .$ _____

9. Add lines 6 through 8 (This is the total of your deductions) . . . .$ _____

10. Subtract line 9 from line 5 (This is you net taxable income) . . . .$ _____

11. Amount of declared tax = 13% of line 10 (Round to the nearest dollar) . . . .$ _____

12. Earned income credit = 7.5% of line 1 (Round to the nearest dollar) . . . . . .$ _____

13. Homestead credit = 12% of line 7 (Round to the nearest dollar) . . . .$ _____

14. Add line 12 and 13 together (Total tax credits) . . . .$ _____

15. Subtract line 14 from line 11 (This is the net declared state tax bill) . . . . . .$ _____

16. Total State income tax withheld . . . .$ _____
(See state withholding statements on W4)

17. If line 16 is larger than line 15, subtract line 15 from line 16.
This is the amount of refund . . . .$ _____

18. If line 15 is larger than line 16, subtract line 16 from line 15.
This is the amount that you still owe . . . .$ _____

Sign Here _____ Date _____

Under penalties of law, I declare that this return and all information are true, correct and complete to the best of my knowledge.

There can be a penalty applied to any tax return that is turned in after the deadline.

12 Real-life Math Projects Kids Will Love   Scholastic Professional Books, 2003

FORM 1040 U.S. Income Tax Return

Income

1. Wages . . . . $ _____

2. Interest on savings . . . . $ _____

3. Interest on CD's . . . . $ _____

4. Dividends from stock . . . . $ _____

5. Add lines 1 through 4 (This is the amount of your taxable income) . . . . $ _____

Deductions

Use Schedule A: Itemized Deductions to calculate these totals

6. Medical and dental expense deduction = ... $ _____

7. Charitable donation deduction = ... $ _____

8. Taxes you paid = ... $ _____

9. Miscellaneous deductions = ... $ _____

10. Add lines 6 through 9 (total itemized deductions). . . . . $ _____

Adjusted Income

11. Subtract line 10 from line 5 (This is your net taxable income.) . . . . $ _____

Tax Computation

12. Amount of declared tax =

Tax rate × Total of line 11 (Round to the nearest dollar) . . . . $ _____

Tax Rate Schedule

If adjusted income is between $0 - $12,000 . . . . = 18% tax rate

If adjusted income is between $12,000 - $40,000 . . . = 24% tax rate

If adjusted income is between $40,000 - $95,000 . . . = 28% tax rate

If adjusted income is over $95,000 . . . . = 33% tax rate

6 2 0 7 4 9 3 7 8 2 0 7 4 9

FORM 1040 U.S. Income Tax Return (cont.)

Tax Credits

13. Dependent credit. Number of children (under 18) = _____ x $500 . . . $ _____

14. Credit for elderly dependent care . . . . $ _____

15. Earned income credit = 4 % of line 1 . . . . $ _____

16. Homestead credit = 10.5 % of line 8 (Itemized deductions) . . . . $ _____
     (Round to the nearest dollar)

17. Add lines 13 through 16 together (Total tax credits) . . . . $ _____

Declared Tax

18. Subtract line 17 from line 12 of Form 1040. . . . . $ _____
     (This is the net declared tax.)

Payments

19. Total Federal income tax withheld . . . . $ _____
     (See Federal withholding statements on W4.)

Refund

20. If line 19 is larger than line 18, subtract line 18 from line 19.

   This is the amount of refund. . . . . $ _____

Amount You Owe

21. If line 18 is larger than line 19, subtract line 19 from line 18.

   This is the amount that you still owe. . . . . $ _____

Sign Here _____   Date _____

Under penalties of law, I declare that this return and all information are true, correct and complete to the best of my knowledge.

There can be a penalty applied to any tax return that is turned in after the deadline.

12 Real-Life Math Projects Kids Will Love   Scholastic Professional Books, 2003

Schedule A: Itemized Deductions

Medical and dental expenses

1. Medical and dental expenses = ...$ _____

2. Multiply line 1 by 76.8 % (Round to the nearest dollar) . . .$ _____

3. Use the line 2 total if line 2 is greater than 12 % of $30,000. Use the minimum deduction of $600 if line 2 is less than 12 % of $30,000.

4. Medical and dental deduction taken . . . .$ _____

Charity and other donations

5. Gifts of money = ...$ _____

6. Gifts of property = ...$ _____

7. Total donations = ...$ _____

8. Use the line 7 total, if line 7 is greater than 6 % of $30,000. Use the minimum deduction of $2,250 if line 7 is less than 6 % of $30,000.

9. Charity and other donations taken . . . .$ _____

Taxes you paid

10. State taxes (Line 15 of the state tax return) = ...$ _____

11. Total property taxes = ...$ _____

12. Add lines 10 and 11. Total other taxes paid = ...$ _____

Miscellaneous deductions

13. Day care costs = ...$ _____

14. Total job expenses = ...$ _____

15. Mortgage interest paid = ...$ _____

16. Retirement investment (IRA) = ...$ _____

17. Add lines 13 through 16 (Total miscellaneous deductions) . . . .$ _____

Total itemized deductions

18. Add lines 4, 9, 12, and 17 . . . .$ _____

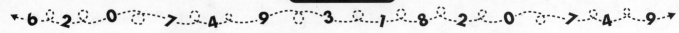
 # Take a Survey

Students assume the role of inventory manager for an athletic shoe store. They conduct a survey on the products they plan to carry and interpret their data to make informed choices as managers.

About the Project

NCTM Standards

Numbers and Number Concepts, Number Systems and Number Theory, Computation and Estimation Patterns and Functions

National Economic Standards

Standard 14

Required Skills

collecting data for a random sample survey
displaying data on a bar graph and circle graph
showing ratios
calculating the percent of a number
adding whole numbers
converting fractions and percents
rounding
constructing angles with a protractor

Materials

reproducibles (pages 57–61)
colored pencils
protractor

Before You Begin

▲ Introduce this project as a challenge to provide a local shoe store owner with the best recommendation about which shoe brands to carry. You can boost students' motivation by having the class select three name brands of shoes to include in their survey. Invite students to brainstorm favorite shoe brands and narrow them down to the three that are most popular. On day 1, students can fill in the chart with the three brands they have chosen for Brand 1, Brand 2, and Brand 3. Have all students use the same three brand names so they can easily compare their survey results.

Lesson Plan

Day 1

Lead a group discussion on the process of conducting a survey, and talk about possible sources of error and bias in results. Be sure to share the following tips for conducting a survey:

• Survey a person only once. If the survey size is twenty people, that means twenty *different* people.

• Avoid steering a person toward a particular answer, for example, "I think basketball shoes are the best, don't you?"

• Survey an equal number of boys and girls, as they may have different interests.

• Keep the survey as random as possible. Surveying people at basketball practice will yield different results than surveying people at lunch. A lunchroom survey offers a better random sample because the surveyor has no control over who might walk by next.

• Record the answers to the survey questions immediately. Surveyors avoid errors in the

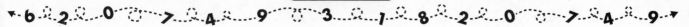
data by making a record on the spot, rather than trying to memorize people's responses and approximating their answers later.

Day 2

Distribute copies of the Take a Survey reproducibles (pages 58–61) and let students prepare their Data Collection Sheet by selecting brand names and determining the survey size. (The survey size for each question can be adjusted to best fit your student population, but should be no higher than thirty students to keep the survey manageable.)

Students may begin to collect their data in class and list places outside of class where they may finish their survey (e.g., before and after school, at lunch, and during study period).

Day 3/4

Let the class review their survey results and complete page 59 to determine the ratios of sneaker preferences of girls to boys. What are some general trends they have found? Can they make any recommendations about what girls and boys want to buy that would help the shoe store owner make good choices for her next order of men's and women's athletic shoes?

Have students work with their Data Collection Sheets and page 60, Circle Graph Display of the Survey Data to figure out the response percentages for each survey question. You might model how to find the response percentage with an example such as: If a survey of 10 students showed that 6 students preferred Nikes and 4 preferred Adidas, then 6 out of 10 (6/10) is .6 or 60% in favor of Nikes and 4 out of 10 (4/10) is .4 or 40% in favor of Adidas.

Once they have made their calculations, they should be able to represent this survey informa-tion on the circle graphs. Your students have two options in completing the circle graphs.

OPTION 1. Students who are less familiar with circle graphs can use estimation to show percentages on the circle graph. They can break the circle up in parts that are easy to determine: 75%, 50%, 25%. If they are graphing 35%, they first create a slice that is 25% and make it just a bit bigger. Their graphs will not be exactly accurate but they will start to understand number relationships on a circle graph.

OPTION 2. Students who are familiar with circle graphs can determine the angle size for a percentage using this equation: The percentage x 360° = The angle size for the circle graph.

Example:
Find and graph the angle size for 35%.
35% = .35 so .35 x 360° = 126°
Use a protractor to draw a 126° angle on the circle graph. Start at the reference line provided on each circle graph and measure a 126° angle.

Students then repeat this process to determine the size of all angles for the circle graph.

When you have corrected students' work and their circle graphs are accurately drawn, invite students to use different colors to make the graphs look attractive for their presentation to the store manager.

Note: Allow younger students to finish their project here and sum up their findings to the store owner in an oral or short written report.

Day 5 (challenging)

Let students work on the Recommended Order Sheet (page 61). Explain that students will show how many of the 500 pairs of shoes should be ordered for each style from each brand and at what price. Post or distribute copies of the Flow Chart for the Recommended Order sheet (page 57) to support your students as they work through the chart. Use the completed example as a reference.

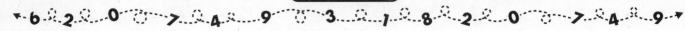
Day 6

Have students complete the Recommended Order Sheet. Circulate to provide support and answer questions as students work.

Day 7

Have students briefly present what they will recommend to the owner. They may create bar graphs that show how many shoes are on their recommended order by brand, by price, and by style.

Day 8

Have students complete the written assessment at the end of this lesson.

TEACHING TIPS

■ **Tally 'em up.** Encourage your students to use tally marks to record results on the Data Collection Sheet. Have them convert these tally marks to a number and record the number in the circle provided. This will make it easier for you to correct.

卌 ||| ⑧

■ **Sometimes it's okay to break the rules!** Point out to students that "breaking the rules" of rounding is sometimes needed to make the percentages come out to 100%. In fact, it is possible to have 99% on a circle graph if you're required to round all the percentages down. For example, 30 students respond to a question about favorite shoe types.

7 say *basketball*: 7/30 = .233
(rounded = 23%)

13 say *cross trainer*: 13/30 = .433
(rounded = 43%)

10 say *running*: 10/30 = .333
(rounded = 33%)

The total percent for these responses represented on a circle graph is 99%, but a circle graph must have 100%. As a result, one of these will need to be rounded up, breaking the traditional rules of rounding. It doesn't matter which one is rounded up, but this produces a small error in the survey results on the graph.

Extend the Lesson

There is an element of error in the results of every survey. Discuss sources of error with your students. These could include dishonest responses, a sample that is too narrow or not random enough, the surveyor's bias, calculation mistakes, duplication of results, and so forth. Take this opportunity to introduce inequalities ($< >$). A survey result of 35 % with a 2% margin of error really means 33% < real percentage < 37%.

Written Assessment

Have students write a persuasive essay in response to the following topic: Another person has conducted the same survey as you. He collected his data at basketball practices, and concluded that 90% of the kids that buy shoes at the mall would buy basketball shoes. Convince the store owner that the other person's information is unreliable and yours is accurate. Explain what sources of error occurred in the above data. Justify your opinions with mathematical evidence. Also explain how the boy-to-girl ratios affect the types of shoes that are stocked in the store.

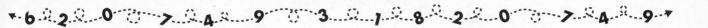

Flow Chart for the Recommended Order Sheet

1. Use the percentages from the survey questions on your circle graph page to fill in the blank lines on the order form with percentage data for style, shoe price, and brands 1, 2, and 3.

2. Begin your calculations in the Number to Order by Style section. Find how many shoes to order of each style (basketball, cross-trainer, and running) by multiplying the percentage of respondents who preferred each style by the total shoe order (500).

Example: Your circle graph shows that 10% of those surveyed preferred basketball shoes. Multiply 10% by 500 (total order). The equation .10 x 500 = 50 tells you that the total number of basketball shoes that you should stock is 50.

Be sure to round your answer to the nearest whole number, and write it in the "Total basketball shoe order" space. Repeat this step to find the total number of cross-trainer and running shoes to order.

3. Find how many basketball shoes to order of each brand. Multiply the "Total basketball shoe order" answer by the percentage for Brands 1, 2, and 3. Be sure to round each answer to the nearest whole number. Write the answers under each brand column in the shaded gray row, "Shoe brand totals" (basketball).

Repeat this step to find the total number of shoes to order of each brand for cross-trainer and running shoes.

4. Find the correct number of Brand 1 basketball shoes to order at each price preference. This tells you, for example, how many Brand 1 basketball shoes should be priced under $40.

Multiply the total number of shoes to order for Brand 1 basketball shoes (gray box) by each price percentage and write the answers in the individual boxes under the Brand 1 column, across from the appropriate price percent.

Repeat this process with Brands 2 and 3 and then for the cross-trainer and running groups.

Example

		(Brand 1) **50** %	(Brand 2) **20** %	(Brand 3) **30** %	Number to Order by Style
	Shoe brand totals ➡	150	60	90	**60** % X 500 preferring basketball
BASKETBALL Preferred shoe prices	under $40 **15** %	22.5 → 23	9	13.5 → 14	
	$40 – $70 **20** %	30	12	18	Total basketball shoe order **300**
	$70 – $100 **40** %	60	24	36	
	over $100 **25** %	37.5 → 37	15	22.5 → 22	
	Shoe brand totals ➡	62.5 or 63	25	37.5 or 37	**25** % X 500 preferring cross-trainer
CROSS-TRAINER Preferred shoe prices	under $40 **15** %	9.45 → 9	3.75 → 4	5.55 → 6	
	$40 – $70 **20** %	12.6 → 13	5	7.4 → 7	Total cross-trainer shoe order **125**
	$70 – $100 **40** %	25.2 → 25	10	14.8 → 15	
	over $100 **25** %	15.75 → 16	6.25 → 6	9.25 → 9	
	Shoe brand totals ➡	37.5 or 38	15	22.5 or 22	**15** % X 500 preferring running
RUNNING Preferred shoe prices	under $40 **15** %	5.7 → 6	2.25 → 2	3.3 → 3	
	$40 – $70 **20** %	7.6 → 8	3	4.4 → 4	Total running shoe order **75**
	$70 – $100 **40** %	15.2 → 15	6	8.8 → 9	
	over $100 **25** %	9.5 → 9	3.75 → 4	5.5 → 6	
Total number of shoes by name brand. (Add up each column.)		251	100	149	Total must equal 500

12 Real-Life Math Projects Kids Will Love Scholastic Professional Books, 2003

6 2 0 7 4 9 3 1 8 2 0 7 4 9

 # Data Collection Sheet

What kinds of shoes do you and your friends like? A new athletic shoe store is coming to the mall, and it's targeting kids your age. You've been hired as the inventory manager, and the owner has asked you to stock 500 pairs of shoes. She suggests that you conduct a survey to determine which types and brands of shoes may sell best. Your task is to collect data, present your findings, and make your recommendations.

Survey Question 1: Survey size = _____ students.

What is your favorite brand of athletic shoe?

Question 1 Data	Brand 1 _____	Brand 2 _____	Brand 3 _____
Girl Responses	⬭	⬭	⬭
Boy Responses	⬭	⬭	⬭
Total Responses	⬭	⬭	⬭

Survey Question 2: Survey size = _____ students.

What price range is the most reasonable for a pair of athletic shoes?

Question 2 Data	Under 40 dollars	40 to 70 dollars	70 to 100 dollars	Over 100 dollars
Girl Responses	⬭	⬭	⬭	⬭
Boy Responses	⬭	⬭	⬭	⬭
Total Responses	⬭	⬭	⬭	⬭

Survey Question 3: Survey size = _____ students.

What type of athletic shoe do you buy most: basketball, cross-trainer, or running?

Question 3 Data	Basketball Shoe	Cross-Trainer Shoe	Running Shoe
Girl Responses	⬭	⬭	⬭
Boy Responses	⬭	⬭	⬭
Total Responses	⬭	⬭	⬭

12 Real-Life Math Projects Kids Will Love Scholastic Professional Books 2003

Ratio Display of the Data

Compare the results of each survey question by giving the information in a ratio of *girls to boys*. Be sure that you write these ratios in their simplest form.

Example: Six girls and ten boys said they buy running shoes most often. You should show the girls-to-boys ratio in any of the following ways: 6:10 or 6 to 10.

Tip: Because $^6/_{10} = {}^3/_5$, the ratio in its simplest form is 3:5 or 3 to 5.

1. _____ girls to boys would buy a pair of Brand 1: _____.

2. _____ girls to boys would buy a pair of Brand 2: _____.

3. _____ girls to boys would buy a pair of Brand 3: _____.

4. _____ girls to boys would buy a pair of shoes priced below 40 dollars.

5. _____ girls to boys would buy a pair of shoes priced below 70 dollars.

6. _____ girls to boys would buy a pair of shoes priced above 70 dollars.

7. _____ girls to boys would buy a pair of basketball shoes.

8. _____ girls to boys would buy a pair of cross-trainer shoes

9. _____ girls to boys would buy a pair of running shoes.

10. _____ girls to boys would buy a pair of running or basketball shoes.

Circle Graph Display of the Survey Data

Create circle graphs to show the results of each survey question. Give all information as a percentage. Round percents to the nearest whole number. Label and color each section of your graphs.

Hint: To find the percent of surveyed people who like Brand 1, divide the total responses for Brand 1 by the total number of people surveyed: Brand 1 responses ÷ Total survey responses.

Survey Question 1

What is you favorite brand of athletic shoe?

Brand 1 _____ = _____ %

Brand 2 _____ = _____ %

Brand 3 _____ = _____ %

Survey Question 2

What price range is the most reasonable for a pair of athletic shoes?
(under $40, $40–$70, $70–$100, over $100)

under $40 = _____ %

$40–$70 = _____ %

$70–$100 = _____ %

over $100 = _____ %

Survey Question 3

What type of athletic shoe do you buy most: basketball, cross-trainer, or running?

Basketball = _____ %

Cross-Trainer = _____ %

Running = _____ %

12 Real-Life Math Projects Kids Will Love Scholastic Professional Books, 2003

Name ______________________________ Date ______________

Recommended Order Sheet

Use your Data Collection Sheet and circle graph percentages to figure out the number of shoes the store owner should order—by name brand, style, and price—for a total order of 500 shoes.

		______ (Brand 1) ____%	______ (Brand 2) ____%	______ (Brand 3) ____%	Number to Order by Style
BASKETBALL	Shoe brand totals →				____% x 500 preferring basketball
Preferred shoe prices	under $40 ____%				
	$40 – $70 ____%				
	$70 – $100 ____%				Total basketball shoe order
	over $100 ____%				______
CROSS-TRAINER	Shoe brand totals →				____% x 500 preferring cross-trainer
Preferred shoe prices	under $40 ____%				
	$40 – $70 ____%				
	$70 – $100 ____%				Total cross-trainer shoe order
	over $100 ____%				______
RUNNING	Shoe brand totals →				____% x 500 preferring running
Preferred shoe prices	under $40 ____%				
	$40 – $70 ____%				
	$70 – $100 ____%				Total running shoe order
	over $100 ____%				______
	Total number of shoes by name brand. (Add up each column.)				→ Total must equal 500

Does your total number of shoes ordered by name brand total 500 pairs of shoes?
YES or NO
If not, find your mistake and change your order if necessary.

What's the Average?

Students calculate the mean, median, and mode from survey data they collect. From this data, they determine which measures of central tendency best represent the average.

About the Project

NCTM Standards

Numbers and Number Relationships, Number Systems and Number Theory, Computation and Estimation, Statistics

Required Skills

survey question development
data collection and display
measures of central tendency
mean, median, mode
rounding
division of whole numbers

Materials

reproducibles (pages 65–67)

Lesson Plan

Day 1

Discuss and define mean, median, and mode with your students. These are called central tendencies—ways of showing how numerical information can be grouped to show an average.

● mean	The average for a set of numbers
● median	The middle number in a set of numbers organized in least-to-greatest order
● mode	The number that occurs most often in a set

Show your students how data can be misleading. Give examples of how one or two numbers in a set of data can "throw off" the mean, which is what most people refer to as the *average*. I usually ask my class, "How many hours a week do you watch TV?" Typically, I get some very high and low numbers. I then ask, "Since we got some high and low numbers, will a mean or average number really represent the amount of time the students on either end of the extreme watch TV?" The class starts to see that the mean doesn't always describe a situation well.

Here's another scenario to demonstrate why the mean doesn't always best describe a set of numbers.

A student has the following test scores in September:
100, 98, 100, 95, 40, 95, 95

The mean of the scores is 89% (score total ÷ 7)
The median is 95% (40, 95, 95, (95), 98, 100, 100)
The mode is 95% (the number that occurs most often in the set)

Typically, we take the mean of the scores to

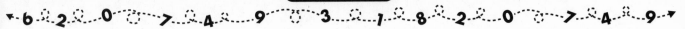
determine how the student usually performs. However, the score of 40% is abnormally low (and not typical for this student). It brings down the mean to a B+ (89%). To say that this student normally earns a B+ on tests is not really true. So, here the median and mode (both 95%) best represent the student's "average" performance.

Distribute copies of page 65, What's the Average? Review the directions with students and demonstrate how to take a survey, using a survey question that the students generate. (Remind students that the question must produce only numeric answers.) Poll the class. Then guide students to calculate the mean, median, and mode from this information. Discuss what central tendency best describes the average.

Day 2

Distribute one copy of the Data Collection sheet (page 66) and three copies of the Survey Data Display sheet (page 67) (one sheet for each question) to every student. Students begin to collect and record their data on the Data Collection Sheet by asking classmates to answer their three survey questions. The survey size for each question can be adjusted to best fit your student population.

Note: To make the activity shorter or less complicated, you may require students to create one or two questions, rather than three.

When students have completed their data collection, have them write their questions at the top of each Survey Data Display sheet. You may need to model how to create a scatter plot graph (students can refer to their task sheet for an example). Your objective is to show them the effectiveness of this format for displaying data. Charts and tables also work, but they don't show information well at a glance. A scatter plot graph highlights clusters of data;

students can circle areas where many points appear close together (e.g., between the 10 and 17 mark on the task sheet cluster graph). Explain that these clusters eliminate **outliers**, or data outside the norm in a set. The clusters are an indication of the central tendency for that set.

Day 3

Have students calculate the mean, median, and mode for each data group and determine which measure of central tendency best describes the average. Have them defend their opinions with a short written response.

Day 4

Have students complete the written assessment at the end of this lesson.

TEACHING TIPS

- **Ask the right questions.** Make sure students have created questions that can only be answered as a numerical quantity. They will find it impossible to work with questions like, "What is your favorite color?" Also, beware of questions like, "What is your favorite number?" or "Rate something from 1 to 10." Although the answers are numbers, the responses are subjective.

Extend the Lesson

There is an old saying, "You can make numbers say anything." Advertisers use statistics to sway the public toward a point of view. Help your students identify bias in data collection and display. Have them look at their results and discuss how they could "trick" people with their data.

For example, the Super Fizz soft drink company conducts a survey to determine how

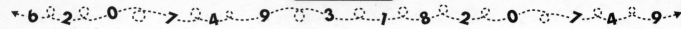
many cans of Super Fizz people drink a week.
One surveyor collects the following data:
2, 3, 35, 4, 3, 4, 5, 40, 2, 2

They use the mean (100 cans /10 people) to
show that people drink an average of 10 cans of
Super Fizz a week. Discuss how the average
would look much less impressive if the
advertiser had used the median or mode.

Written Assessment

Pose the following prompt to students: Is there
ever a time that the average isn't average? After
completing this survey project, a classmate
claims that the average person makes 7 phone
calls per week, and shows you the following
survey responses:
(1, 2, 3, 3, 4, 4, 5, 5, 5, 5, 5, 5, 5, 8, 45)
Your classmate is correct; the mean for this set
of numbers is 7. Support a different conclusion
about the average number of phone calls your
classmates make. Defend your conclusion with
information from this same set of data.

What's the Average?

What's the average number of students in a class at your school? How would you figure it out? There are three different ways to determine average: mean, median, and mode. You're going to look at three categories and use these methods to determine what is *average* among your peers.

Your Task

1. Create three interesting survey questions for your peers to answer. Phrase your questions so the only answer possible is a number.

2. Survey your classmates and record their responses on the Data Collection sheet. You will be asking 15 peers question one, 20 peers question two, and 25 peers question three.

3. Create a scatter plot graph and determine the mean, median, and mode for each survey question. Show your work so you can quickly find and correct mistakes.

4. Determine which measure of central tendency (mean, median, or mode) best shows the average among your peers.

Example

Survey Question: How many CDs do you own? (seven people surveyed)

Results:

Peer responses: 15, 10, 13, 2, 14, 17,10

Create a scatter plot graph that displays your results. Draw a ring around the points that are most closely grouped together.

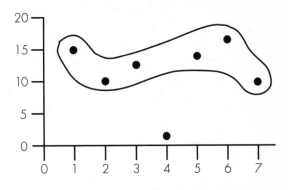

What is the **mean** of your data? Remember to round to the nearest whole number when you get a decimal answer.

2 + 10 + 10 + 13 + 14 + 15 + 17 = 81
81 ÷ 7 = 11.571
Mean = 12

Most data is clustered between 10 and 17. The point outside this cluster, 2, is called an **outlier**. Outliers are data outside the norm. The scatter plot graph shows that the "average" or central tendency would be between 10 and 17.

List your results in least-to-greatest order and then identify the **median** for your data.

2, 10, 10, (13), 14, 15, 17   Median = 13

What is the **mode**?

Mode = 10 (The number 10 occurs most often in this set)

6 2 0 7 4 9 3 1 8 2 0 7 4 9

🖍 Data Collection 🖍

Write your survey questions below. Use the space under each question to record your survey data.

Question One _____

_____

Use the space below to collect the data from question one. (15 peers surveyed)

Question Two _____

_____

Use the space below to collect the data from question two. (20 peers surveyed)

Question Three _____

_____

Use the space below to collect the data from question three. (25 peers surveyed)

12 Real-life Math Projects Kids Will Love Scholastic Professional Books, 2003

Survey Data Display

Use the data you gathered from your Data Collection sheet to show your results for one survey question.

Survey Question: _____

_____

Results: Create a scatter plot graph that best displays your results of 15, 20, or 25 peers surveyed.

What is the **mean** for your data? (Round to the nearest whole number when you get a decimal answer.)

List your results in least-to-greatest order and then identify the **median** of your data.

What is the **mode** of your data?

What measure of central tendency best describes your data as "average": mean, median, or mode? Defend your opinion with a short explanation.

_____

_____

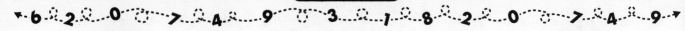

Take Your Best Guess

Students use a random sample to make predictions about the number of colored marbles in a container.

▲▲▲▲▲▲▲▲▲▲▲▲▲▲▲▲▲

About the Project

▼▼▼▼▼▼▼▼▼▼▼▼▼▼▼▼

NCTM Standards

Numbers and Number Concepts, Number Systems and Number Theory, Computation and Estimation, Patterns and Functions, Statistics, Probability

National Economic Standards

Standard 4

Required Skills

determine a probability fraction and percentage
statistical projections
multiplying decimals
rounding
making inferences and drawing conclusions

Materials

reproducibles (pages 70–72)
coffee can
500 marbles (200 blue, 150 yellow, 100 black, 45 white, 5 gold, 0 green)
(If you substitute other colors, keep a record of the number of each color.)

▲▲▲▲▲▲▲▲▲▲▲▲▲▲▲▲

Lesson Plan

▼▼▼▼▼▼▼▼▼▼▼▼▼▼▼▼

Day 1

Show your students the can of marbles and ask them what they could infer about the contents if you showed them some, but not all, of the marbles. Build a discussion from any responses that recommend sampling. Explain *random sampling*, and how it might be used to determine the colors and amounts of marbles in the can. (For this project, tell students that random sampling means selecting a set of marbles without looking into the can.)

Distribute copies of pages 70–72 and review the probability challenge: Can students use their math skills to predict how many marbles of each color are in the can? Based on their knowledge of the total sample (500 marbles), have students use the following equation to form their predictions of how many marbles of each color are in the can:

Probability fraction or decimal x 500 = Expected outcome

Review the example on page 70, making sure to highlight these points:

• The probability fraction is the number of each marble chosen over the total marbles in the sample. For example, if 10 white marbles are chosen out of a sample of 25, the probability fraction for a white marble equals $10/25$ or $2/5$.

• These equations can be solved using fractions or decimals. On each table, students will find a place to convert the probability fraction to a probability decimal. For example, $2/5 = .4$. Let students know what you will require.

• The expected *outcome* or result is the total number of a certain colored marble you would expect to find in the can of 500 marbles. If

your probability fraction for a white marble is $2/5$, then $2/5 \times 500 = 200$ white marbles or $.4 \times 500 = 200$ white marbles.

Conduct Sample 1 with your students (a 25-marble sample). Have them make calculations and determine the expected outcomes.

Day 2

Conduct Sample 2 with your students (a 75-marble sample). Have them complete both Sample 2 and the combined sample on page 71. Explain that combined samples will give a more accurate prediction because they represent a larger set of the whole than the individual samples.

Day 3

Conduct Sample 3 with your students (a 125-marble sample). Have them complete both Sample 3 and the combined sample on page 72. When students have finished, reveal the actual number of marbles of each color and discuss the accuracy of their predictions.

Day 4

Have students complete the written assessment at the end of the lesson.

TEACHING TIPS

- **Find marbles.** You can purchase colored marbles at any craft or hobby store. Look for decorative colored marbles used in vases or fish tanks.

- **Discuss independent probability.** This project uses independent probability, which means that every marble selection must occur with the same variables. Make sure to point out that it's important to return each marble after choosing it from the can. Leaving even one marble out will change the

probability for the next marble that is selected since there will be only 499 marbles in the can, not the standard 500.

- **Involve students in tallying results.** Students like to keep track of the marbles as you pick them. Choose a few students from your class to keep a record of the sample results. Have one student keep track of the total number of picks and have another student tally the number chosen for each color (white, yellow, blue, green, gold, black). They can record these totals on the chalkboard or in a notebook.

Extend the Lesson

Discuss with your students the difference between the expected outcome and real outcome in taking a sample. For example, it is possible to select a gold marble every time for five consecutive turns, but because the gold marble has a low probability of being picked ($5/500$ or 1%), this is not expected to happen. Similarly, it would be possible to flip a coin 100 times and get 100 heads, but the odds against such an occurrence are astronomical.

Discuss with students how the size of the sample affects the quality of their prediction. Ask them, "What sample sizes would give you the best information?" They should conclude that the larger the sample size is, the more reliable their predictions will be.

Written Assessment

Have students respond to this statement: The Department of Natural Resources says that there are 1,500,000 wild deer in your state. It is impossible to go into all of the wild areas and farmland of your state to count every deer. Explain how the Department of Natural Resources could use sampling to determine the number of wild deer.

Take Your Best Guess

Can you guess how many white marbles are in the can? There are a total of 500 marbles—some white, yellow, blue, green, gold, and black. But what colors are they and how many are there of each color? You are not allowed to see all of them but you can find out a lot by taking samples. We'll pick a random sample of marbles from the can. From this sample, you'll find the probability fraction for each color chosen and predict how many marbles of each color are in the can.

Example: 25 marbles are chosen for Sample 1.

- You can determine the probability fraction for white marbles. It is the number of white marbles chosen over the total marbles in the sample. If 10 white marbles are chosen out of a sample of 25 marbles, the probability fraction for a white marble equals $^{10}/_{25}$ or $^2/_5$.

- You have the option of solving these equations using fractions or decimals. The Probability decimal column in each table gives you a place to convert the probability fraction to a probability decimal. For example, $^2/_5 = .4$

- The expected outcome is the total number of colored marbles you would expect to find in the can of 500 marbles. If your probability fraction for a white marble is $^2/_5$, then $^2/_5 \times 500 = 200$ white marbles or $.4 \times 500 = 200$ white marbles.

- Repeat this process to determine the expected outcomes for the other colored marbles.

Sample 1   Number of marbles taken in this sample = ___ marbles.

Marble Color	Amount Chosen From the Sample	Probability Fraction (reduce to lowest terms)	Probability Decimal (round to the nearest hundredth)	Expected Outcome (round to the nearest whole number)
White				
Yellow				
Blue				
Green				
Gold				
Black				

12 Real-Life Math Projects Kids Will Love   Scholastic Professional Books, 2003

Sample 2   Number of marbles taken in this sample = ___ marbles.

Marble Color	Amount Chosen From the Sample	Probability Fraction (reduce to lowest terms)	Probability Decimal (round to the nearest hundredth)	Expected Outcome (round to the nearest whole number)
White				
Yellow				
Blue				
Green				
Gold				
Black				

Combine Samples 1 and 2

Total number of marbles taken by combining Samples 1 and 2 = ___ marbles.
Determine the amounts for this table from the combined samples.

Marble Color	Amount Chosen From the Sample	Probability Fraction (reduce to lowest terms)	Probability Decimal (round to the nearest hundredth)	Expected Outcome (round to the nearest whole number)
White				
Yellow				
Blue				
Green				
Gold				
Black				

Name _____ Date _____

Sample 3   Number of marbles taken in this sample = ___ marbles.

Marble Color	Amount Chosen From the Sample	Probability Fraction (reduce to lowest terms)	Probability Decimal (round to the nearest hundredth)	Expected Outcome (round to the nearest whole number)
White				
Yellow				
Blue				
Green				
Gold				
Black				

Combine Samples 1, 2, and 3.

Total number of marbles taken by combining Samples 1, 2, and 3 = ___ marbles.
Determine the amounts for this table from the combined samples.

Marble Color	Amount Chosen From the Sample	Probability Fraction (reduce to lowest terms)	Probability Decimal (round to the nearest hundredth)	Expected Outcome (round to the nearest whole number)
White				
Yellow				
Blue				
Green				
Gold				
Black				

How accurate are you? The actual amounts will be given at the end of the project, after you've taken all three samples and made your predictions. Use the information from the samples to see how close you came in predicting the actual amounts. There are 500 marbles in the jar. The actual totals are:

_____ White _____ Yellow _____ Blue _____ Green _____ Gold _____ Black

12 Real-Life Math Projects Kids Will Love   Scholastic Professional Books, 2003

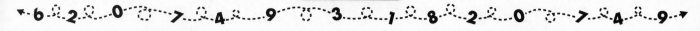
Games of Chance

Students evaluate games of chance for probability and fairness.
They create a tree diagram of possible outcomes and determine real outcomes.
Students also use an equation to determine the expected outcome.

About the Project

NCTM Standards

Numbers and Number Concepts, Number
Systems and Number Theory, Computation
and Estimation, Patterns and Functions,
Probability

Required Skills

determine a probability fraction
show possible outcomes
create a tree diagram for a probability
    simulation
calculate expected outcomes

Materials

reproducibles (pages 76–80)
dice or numbered cubes
coins or chips that can be flipped

Lesson Plan

Day 1

Introduce this project by doing a quick
probability game with your class. Ask your
students to predict the result of a coin flip.
Some will say heads, others will say tails. Then
flip the coin again and discuss the results of
two flips—did it happen the way students
thought it might? Ask students why they
think the coin toss is often used to determine
taking turns in sports or for other decisions

that require an unbiased outcome. This
initiates a discussion of how a practice like
the coin toss can be a fair way to make an
unbiased decision.

Distribute the Games of Chance reproducibles
and have students look at page 76 (class
demonstration page). Tell them that they will
get to play five games of chance and determine
which ones are fair and which are not.

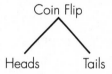

Coin Flip

Heads   Tails

Review the coin toss game, leading them
through the class demonstration section. To
play the game, split your class into two
groups—the group that chose heads and the
group that chose tails. Complete the tree
diagram with students to show that heads and
tails are the possible outcomes to this game.
Ask the groups what the probability fraction
is for each outcome. (Because neither heads
nor tails is guaranteed, the probability fraction
for each outcome is $1/2$—one probable win
for every two tosses.) Demonstrate expected
outcome by flipping the coin ten times. The
expected outcome that the coin will land heads
up five times and tails up five times can be
shown in this equation: Expected outcome for
heads = $1/2$ x 10 tosses. So the expected outcome for the coin to land on each side is 5.

Guide students through questions 1 through 4
on page 76 (for answers, see page 75).

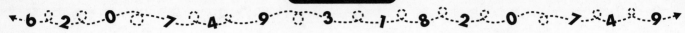
Before students try Game 1, make sure they are familiar with the following vocabulary:

• game of chance	A game where no player can affect the outcome
• fair game	A game where each player has an equal probability of winning
• unfair game	A game where each player has an unequal probability of winning
• probability fraction	The likely outcome over total possible outcomes
• expected outcome	The expected result of playing a probability game (Expected outcome = Probability fraction x Number of times the game is played.)
• real outcome	The actual outcome of a probability game

Have students work in pairs to complete Game 1 (page 77). Leave time at the end of the class period to review the results of the game and make sure students grasp how to list possible outcomes, show probability fractions, and determine whether the game is fair.

Day 2

Have students work in pairs to complete Game 2 and Game 3 (pages 78–79).

Day 3

Students complete Game 4 (page 80) and create their own game of chance. They may also complete the written assessment at the end of this lesson.

TEACHING TIPS

■ **Chance or skill?** Students sometimes confuse games of chance with games of skill. Explain that in a game of chance, no one can control the outcome. Flipping a coin is a game of chance; you can't control whether it lands heads or tails. The outcome of a game of skill, on the other hand, is determined by the ability of the players. Shooting a basketball through a hoop is a game of skill; you have control over whether it goes in or not.

■ **Encourage pair work.** Students usually work best in pairs of two on this project. Each student needs a partner to complete the game simulations.

■ **Don't forget to count "no winner" outcomes!** A common error students make in probability calculations is not accounting for times in a game when there is no winner. For example, in Game 3, a numbered die is rolled once. You win if the number is prime. Your opponent wins if the number is composite. Students assume this game is fair because there are three prime numbers and 6 possible outcomes. They often fail to see that the number one is neither prime nor composite, and as a result there is no winner with the number one. This game is unfair because one player has a $1/2$ probability of winning and the other player has $1/3$ probability. There is a $1/6$ probability that there will be no winner.

Extend the Lesson

Highlight the difference between the expected outcome and real outcome by playing an extended probability game. It is possible to flip a coin 100 times and get 100 heads, but it would not be expected to happen. What are students' predictions and what is the real outcome?

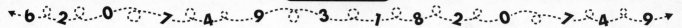
Written Assessment

Write a response to the following statement: You have a bag that contains different colors of marbles. The bag contains 10 blue marbles, 12 yellow marbles, and 8 red marbles. How can you make the probability of choosing a blue marble $1/2$ without adding any marbles to the bag?

Answer Key

Page 76

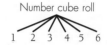

Coin Flip

Heads   Tails

Possible Outcomes: (Heads), (Tails)
Probability Fraction:
P(heads) = $1/2$
P(tails) = $1/2$
1. Fair
2. The probability fraction for each outcome, heads and tails, is equal.
3. There should be 5 head outcomes (10 x $1/2$ = 5); There should be 5 tail outcomes (10 x $1/2$ = 5).
4. Answers will vary. (Students should report on the real outcome, e.g., "We tossed the coin 10 times. Heads came up 7 times and tails came up 3 times.")

Page 77

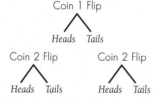

Coin 1 Flip

Heads   Tails

Coin 2 Flip   Coin 2 Flip

Heads   Tails   Heads   Tails

Possible Outcomes: (Heads, Heads); (Heads, Tails); (Tails, Tails); (Tails, Heads)
Probability Fraction:
P(same) = $2/4$ or $1/2$ (opponent wins)
P(different) = $2/4$ or $1/2$ (you win)
1. Fair
2. The probability fraction for each outcome, same and different, is equal.
3. There should be 10 same outcomes (20 x $1/2$ = 10); There should be 10 different outcomes (20 x $1/2$ = 10).
4. Answers will vary.

Page 78

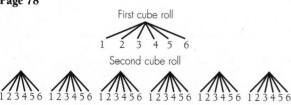

First cube roll

1 2 3 4 5 6

Second cube roll

123456 123456 123456 123456 123456 123456

Possible Outcomes:

(1,1)	(1,2)	(1,3)	(1,4)	(1,5)	(1,6)
(2,1)	(2,2)	(2,3)	(2,4)	(2,5)	(2,6)
(3,1)	(3,2)	(3,3)	(3,4)	(3,5)	(3,6)
(4,1)	(4,2)	(4,3)	(4,4)	(4,5)	(4,6)
(5,1)	(5,2)	(5,3)	(5,4)	(5,5)	(5,6)
(6,1)	(6,2)	(6,3)	(6,4)	(6,5)	(6,6)

Probability Fraction:
P(sum < 7) = $15/36$ or $5/12$ (opponent wins)
P(sum > 7) = $15/36$ or $5/12$ (you win)
P(sum = 7) = $6/36$ or $1/6$ (no winner)
1. Fair
2. The probability fraction for outcomes where I win and the probability fraction where my opponent wins are equal.
3. There should be 5 (sum < 7) outcomes (12 x $5/12$ = 5); There should be 5 (sum > 7) outcomes (12 x $5/12$ = 5); There should be 2 (sum = 7) outcomes (12 x $1/6$ = 2)
4. Answers will vary.

Page 79

Number cube roll

1   2   3   4   5   6

Possible Outcomes: (1), (2), (3), (4), (5), (6)

Probability Fraction:
P(prime) = $3/6$ or $1/2$ (opponent wins)
P(composite) = $2/6$ or $1/3$ (you win)
P(Neither) = $1/6$ (no winner)
1. Unfair
2. The probability fraction for outcomes where I win and the probability fraction where my opponent wins are not equal.
3. There should be 9 prime outcomes (18 x $1/2$ = 9); There should be 6 composite outcomes (18 x $1/3$ = 6); There should be 3 no winner (1) outcomes (18 x $1/6$ = 3)
4. Answers will vary.

Page 80

Possible Outcomes:

(R,R)	(R,P)	(R,S)
(P,R)	(P,P)	(P,S)
(S,R)	(S,P)	(S,S)

Player 1

R   P   S

Player 2

R P S   R P S   R P S

Probability Fraction:
P(you win) = $3/9$ or $1/3$
P(opponent wins) = $3/9$ or $1/3$
P(no winner) = $3/9$ or $1/3$
1. Fair
2. The probability fraction for outcomes where I win and the probability fraction where my opponent wins are equal.
3. There should be 6 "I win" outcomes (18 x $1/3$ = 6); There should be 6 "my opponent wins" outcomes (18 x $1/3$ = 6); There should be 6 "no winner" outcomes (18 x $1/3$ = 6).
4. Answers will vary.

Games of Chance

Flip a coin. Will it be heads or tails? You make the choice. You may think the odds are equal, but how do you know? Below are four games of chance. Some are fair and some are unfair. Which ones would you want to play? Do the following to help you evaluate each game:

- Draw a tree diagram showing all possible outcomes.
- Find the probability fraction for each outcome.
- Determine if the game is fair or unfair.
- Calculate the expected outcome for each possible outcome.
- Expected outcome = probability fraction x number of times the game is played
- Perform a game simulation.
- Write about the real outcome of the game simulation.

Class Demonstration

A coin is tossed. You win if the coin lands heads up and your opponent wins if the coin lands tails up.

Tree Diagram

Coin Flip

Possible Outcomes

List each possible outcome.

_____

_____

Probability Fraction

Determine the probabilities of the coin landing heads up and tails up.

P(heads) = _____

P(tails) = _____

1. Is this a fair or unfair game? _____

2. What is the reason you believe this? _____

_____

3. Play the game! Flip a coin 10 times.

What do you predict will happen? Calculate the expected outcome for each possible outcome.

Expected outcome = Probability fraction x Number of times the game is played

_____

_____

4. What was the real outcome when you played the game?

_____

12 Real-life Math Projects Kids Will Love Scholastic Professional Books, 2003

Games of Chance: Game One

Two coins are tossed at the same time. You win if the coins are different (example: heads, tails) and your opponent wins if the two coins are the same (example: tails, tails).

Tree Diagram

Coin Flip

Coin Flip    Coin Flip

Possible Outcomes
List each possible outcome.
_____
_____
_____
_____

Probability Fraction
Determine the probabilities of the coin landing heads up and tails up.

P(same)   = _____ (opponent wins)

P(different) = _____ (you win)

1. Is this a fair or unfair game? _____

2. What is the reason you believe this?

_____

3. Play the game! Flip a coin 20 times.

What do you predict will happen? Calculate the expected outcomes for the coin flip results being a) the same and b) different.

Expected outcome = Probability fraction x Number of times the game is played

_____

_____

4. What was the real outcome when you played the game?

_____

_____

_____

Games of Chance: Game Two

A numbered cube (a die with sides 1, 2, 3, 4, 5, and 6) is rolled twice. You win if the sum of the numbers is *less than 7*. Your opponent wins if the sum of the numbers is *greater than 7*.

Tree Diagram

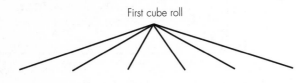

First cube roll

Second cube roll

Possible Outcomes

List each possible outcome.

_____

_____

_____

_____

_____

_____

Probability Fraction

Determine the probabilities for the numbered cube sums.

P(sum < 7) = _____ (opponent wins)

P(sum > 7) = _____ (you win)

P(sum > 7) = _____ (no winner)

1. Is this a fair or unfair game? _____

2. What is the reason you believe this?

_____

3. Play the game! Role a die 12 times.

What do you predict will happen? Calculate the expected outcome for the sum of the cubes < 7, the sum of the cubes > 7, and the sum of the cubes = 7.

Expected outcome = Probability fraction x Number of times the game is played

_____

_____

4. What was the real outcome when you played the game?

_____

_____

_____

12 Real-Life Math Projects Kids Will Love Scholastic Professional Books, 2003

6 2 0 7 4 9 3 7 8 2 0 7 4 9

Games of Chance: Game Three

A numbered cube (a die with sides 1, 2, 3, 4, 5, and 6) is rolled. You win if the number rolled is composite (4, 6). Your opponent wins is the number rolled is prime (2, 3, 5).

Tree Diagram

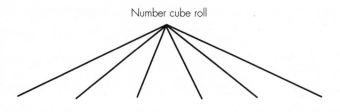

Number cube roll

1. Is this a fair or unfair game? _____

2. What is the reason you believe this?

_____

_____

Possible Outcomes
List each possible outcome.

_____

_____

_____

Probability Fraction
Determine the probabilities of the numbered cube landing on a prime number, composite number, or neither. The number 1 is neither prime nor composite.

P(prime)   = _____ (opponent wins)

P(composite) = _____ (you win)

P(neither)   = _____ (no winner)

3. Play the game! Role a die 18 times.

What do you predict will happen? Calculate the expected outcome for the die landing on a prime number, composite number, or neither. The number 1 is neither prime nor composite.

Expected outcome = Probability fraction x Number of times the game is played

_____

_____

4. What was the real outcome when you played the game?

_____

_____

_____

Games of Chance: Game Four

Rock, Paper, Scissors is a game played by two people. On a turn, both players make a hand gesture on the count of three. The players may show one of three gestures—a fist to show a rock, an open hand to show paper, or a "V" with their fingers to show scissors.

The winner of the game is determined by which gesture each person chooses. If paper and rock are chosen, then paper wins because paper covers rock. If paper and scissors are chosen, scissors wins because scissors cuts paper. If rock and scissors are chosen, rock wins because scissors can't cut rock. There is no winner when both people choose the same thing. Use the following abbreviation when making your tree diagram: R—rock, P—paper, S—scissors.

Possible Outcomes

List each possible outcome.

_____

_____

_____

Probability Fraction

Determine the probabilities of you winning, your opponent winning, and there being no winner.

P(you win)   = _____

P(opponent wins) = _____

P(no winner)   = _____

Tree Diagram

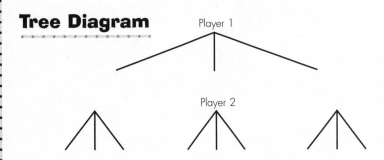

1. Is this a fair or unfair game? _____

2. What is the reason you believe this?

_____

3. Play the game! Play Rock, Paper, Scissors with a partner 18 times.

What do you predict will happen? Calculate the expected outcome for you being the winner, for your opponent being the winner, and there being no winner.

Expected outcome = Probability fraction x Number of times the game is played

_____

_____

4. What was the real outcome when you played the game?

_____

_____

12 Real-Life Math Projects Kids Will Love Scholastic Professional Books, 2003

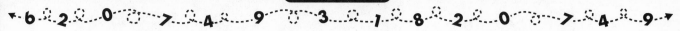
 # Home Design Project

(challenging)

Students design and draw a scale floor plan for a ranch home.
They calculate square footage and all associated costs.

About the Project

NCTM Standards

Numbers and Number Relationships, Number Systems and Number Theory, Computation and Estimation, Geometry, Measurement, Algebra

National Economic Standards

Standard 2

Required Skills

measuring in square feet
drawing to scale
finding area and perimeter of geometric shapes
multiplication of whole numbers
rounding
inequalities

Materials

reproducibles (pages 84–87)
architectural blueprints or home design
  magazines with floor plan renderings

Before You Begin

▲ This is a fun but sophisticated lesson that requires students to work with the concept of square units of measure in creating the rooms and spaces of a dream home. If students are not familiar with square footage and how the area of a room is represented in a scale drawing, they will need practice measuring physical spaces to determine square footage, as well as showing that measurement in a scale drawing on grid paper. The scale used in this project is 2 feet = $1/4$ inch ($1/4$-inch grid paper is used).

Lesson Plan

Day 1

Ask students what their dream homes would look like and let them start to compare details, size, space ideas, and so on. Share architectural blueprints or floor plan drawings from home design magazines to spark their interest and imagination. When students have had a chance to brainstorm, tell them that they are going to play the role of architect in a project that gives them a chance to design their own dream homes.

As students talk about the size of their dream homes, review square footage, the key unit of measure architects use to plan space. It is the unit which students will use in their projects to show the size of the rooms in and outdoor spaces around their houses. Explain that available money and building codes (restrictions or requirements about what can be included in a new building) play a big role in the way architects design a house.

Distribute copies of pages 84 (Home Design Project task page) and introduce students to the details of the assignment—a chance to design their very own one-story home.

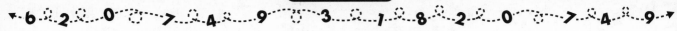

Explain that while they will be given many choices in designing the space, they will be required to follow the building codes listed on page 84. Review with students each of the building codes, answering any questions that come up. Discuss the required items and options that can be included in the home. Have them reread the assignment and think about how they want to create the space according to the guidelines.

Day 2

Distribute copies of pages 85–87. Using the grid paper, students can practice drawing the geometric shapes listed on the bottom of page 85. Review how to calculate the area of geometric objects (formulas are listed at the bottom of page 85). Then review how to draw rooms and spaces to scale using the grid paper and the scale 2 feet = $1/4$ inch.

Make sure students have a set of symbols to use for their floor plan drawings. (You might want to generate symbols as a class for all the elements listed at the bottom of page 84.) Let students sketch out a rough-draft floor plan for their dream home on another sheet of $1/4$-inch grid paper.

Day 3

Have students refer to the building codes on page 84 and complete a rough draft of the Home Design Worksheet (pages 85–86) to determine whether the home they've sketched is too large or too small and whether it fits the parameters of the building codes and the budget. Make sure students also determine whether the various options they've chosen are financially possible (see options and cost list at the top of page 86).

Days 4 and 5

Now that students understand how the limitations of budget and building code requirements affect their design plans, they are ready to revise their floor plans to meet code and cost specifications. Distribute a second set of copies of pages 85–87 to students and allow them time to revise and redesign their rough sketches as needed.

Day 6

Students complete the final draft of the floor plan. All walls and rooms need to be labeled with dimension sizes. If it is neat enough, they may work off of their revised sketch. Otherwise, they should transfer the design to a fresh sheet of grid paper and add labels and details to the new copy.

Day 7

Students may complete the written assessment at the end of this lesson. Encourage students to create a brochure or advertisement for their home.

TEACHING TIPS

- **Draw what you know.** If your students have a hard time getting started with what to draw, encourage them to start by drawing the floor plan of the home they live in now. This gives them a concrete model to follow.

- **Act as a building inspector.** Your role is that of building inspector. Identify students' design problems and building code violations as their drawings progress. Suggest possible solutions, but allow students to problem-solve on their own as much as possible.

■ **Make enough copies.** I've found that my students make many revisions to their drawings, home design worksheets, and cost calculation sheets before creating a plan that they're happy with. Make sure to run off multiple copies of pages 85–87 for their use.

■ **Emphasize presentation.** Stress to your class that final drawings must be neat and match all the dimensions used on the Home Design Worksheet. The length of all walls must be labeled, options must be chosen and rooms must be named.

■ **Make allowances for irregularly-shaped rooms.** The dimensions of irregularly-shaped rooms do not need to be on the Home Design Worksheet. You can confirm the accuracy of square footage by comparing the area with the dimensions shown on your students' drawings.

■ **Offer high-tech options.** Some students may ask if they can use a CAD program or drafting paper to produce their drawings. If this technology and tech support is available at your school, this project is a perfect opportunity to incorporate technology and math.

Extend the Lesson

Explore surface area of three-dimensional objects. Have your students build a three-dimensional model of their home using tag board. Have them calculate how much area the siding covers.

Explore interest rates and compound interest with your students. Have your students calculate the monthly payments for their home at various interest rates. They can calculate payments using 10-, 15-, or 30-year loans.

Written Assessment

Offer students the following prompt: Create a classified advertisement that gives a brief description of your home. This should include special features, options, and reasons why a person may want to purchase your home.

Home Design Project

What does your dream home look like? Here's your chance to design your very own one-story ranch home! Draw the floor plan to scale. The list of building codes below tells you what rooms and spaces you must include and the budget you'll need to stick to. You may choose additional design features such as a deck or air-conditioning in your plan, but make sure you have enough money in the budget to afford them. You're also going to design your yard, including a driveway and a garden.

Before you begin your first sketch, review all building codes (rules) below. At the bottom of the page, sketch the symbols you will use in your floor plan.

Building Codes

1. Your home must be between 1,400 and 2,000 square feet in size.
- Square footage is calculated from all rooms and hallways (closets are not included).
- The home must have six closets (all closets must be between 8 and 36 square feet in size).
- No room can be smaller than 60 square feet.

2. The attached garage must be between 600 and 1,000 square feet.

3. Your home must have three bedrooms, one kitchen, one dining room, one living room, and two bathrooms.
- Your home can have one bonus room. (Examples: bedroom four, family room)
- Include only the rooms that are listed—no more, no less.

4. All hallways must be exactly four feet wide.

5. Your home must have a driveway, pool, and a garden.

6. The garden must have a fence around its perimeter.
- The area of the garden must be between 20 and 80 square feet

7. The pool must be round and between 100 and 400 square feet. Round off the square footage to the nearest foot.

8. If a deck is added, it must be between 100 and 300 square feet.

9. If a pool and deck are added, the pool must be totally outside the perimeter of the deck.

10. If a hot tub and deck are added, the hot tub must be totally inside the perimeter of the deck.

11. When you choose options, you may not have more than one of each option. (Example: 2 fireplaces)

12. The entire project must cost between $130,000 and $160,000.

13. Each graph square on your grid paper equals two feet by two feet. Use these dimensions to draw the blueprint of your home.

Symbols to Use in the Drawing

Window	Door	Fireplace	Wall, deck, driveway, and fence	Closet
Satellite dish	Central-air unit	Hot tub	Sliding glass doors	Pool

12 Real-Life Math Projects Kids Will Love Scholastic Professional Books, 2003

Home Design Worksheet

Use your floor-plan drawing to calculate square footage of the rooms in your house. The equations at the bottom of the page can help you find the area.

Then figure out how much your design costs, using your plan and the cost lists on the next page.

Square Footage

Room Name	Length	x	Width	=	Area (square feet)
Living Room		x		=	
Dining Room		x		=	
Kitchen		x		=	
Bedroom one		x		=	
Bedroom two		x		=	
Bedroom three		x		=	
Bathroom one		x		=	
Bathroom two		x		=	
All hallways	No dimensions needed			=	
Bonus room (if used)		x		=	
Total square footage				=	

What if my room is not a rectangle?

Leave the length and width dimensions blank for the hallways and any irregularly-shaped rooms. Be sure to fill in the square footage.

Mathematic equations used to calculate square feet

Area of a circle = pi x r^2 (radius squared) (use 3.14 for pi)

Area of a square = length x width

Area of a rectangle = length x width

Area of a trapezoid = [(base 1 + base 2) x height] ÷ 2

Area of a triangle = (base x height) ÷ 2

Mathematic equations used to calculate perimeter

Circumference of a circle = pi x D (diameter) (use 3.14 for pi)

Perimeter of a square = side + side + side + side

Perimeter of a rectangle = side + side + side + side

Perimeter of a trapezoid = side + side + side + side

Perimeter of a triangle = side + side + side

6 2 0 7 4 9 3 1 8 2 0 7 4 9

Home Cost Calculation

Costs of Required Items

Cost of home . . . .$75 per square foot
Cost of garage . . . . $10 per square foot
Cost of pool . . . .$11 per square foot
Driveway . . . .(gravel = $550;
        blacktop = $1,200; cement = $2,250)
Fence . . . .(wood = $9 per foot;
        metal = $7 per foot)

Costs of Options

Deck . . . .$9 per square foot
Fireplace $2,350
Central air-conditioning $1,300
Hot tub $5,500
        (diameter = 8 feet)
Satellite dish $3,150

Your Option Costs

List all options, and their prices used in your home. Leave this section blank if you choose not to include any options in the design of your home.

1. _____ = $ _____
2. _____ = $ _____
3. _____ = $ _____
4. _____ = $ _____
5. _____ = $ _____

Total cost of all options   = $ _____

Deck Calculations

Dimensions of the deck _____ x _____

Total square footage of the deck = _____

Total cost of the deck = $ _____

Your Home Plan Costs: Required Elements

Dimensions of the garden   _____ x _____

Perimeter of the garden   _____ x _____

Type of fence: wood or metal   Cost of fence = $ _____
        (Circle one)

Diameter of the pool   _____

Square footage of the pool   _____   Cost of pool = $ _____
(Round off the nearest whole number)

Dimensions of the garage   _____ x _____

Square footage of the garage   _____   Cost of garage = $ _____

Type of driveway: gravel blacktop cement   Cost of driveway = $ _____
        (circle one)

Total square footage of your home _____   Cost of home = $ _____

                                Total cost of all options = $ _____

Grand total of the entire project = $ _____

12 Real-life Math Projects Kids Will Love   Scholastic Professional Books, 2003

Drawing Paper

Each graph square on your grid paper equals 2 feet by 2 feet.

Use this to sketch a scale drawing of your home.

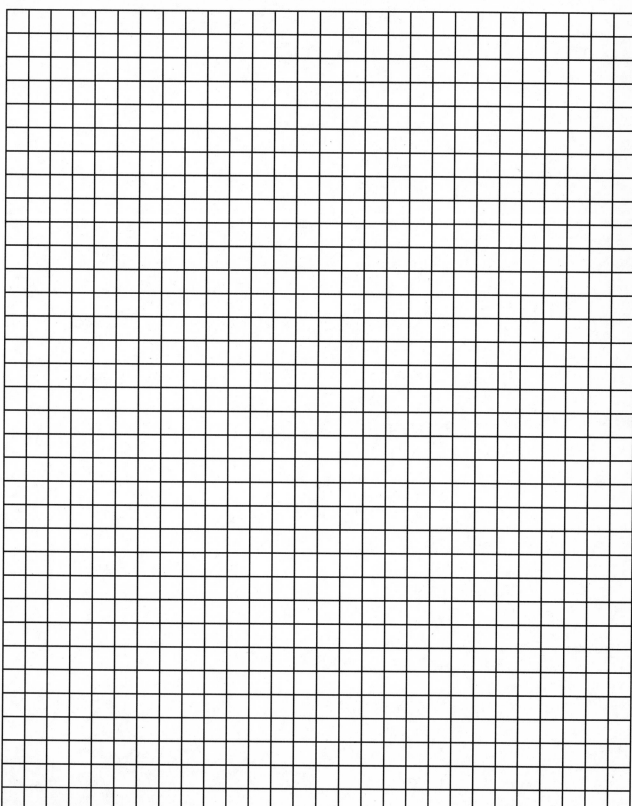

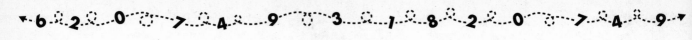

Notes